ABOUT THIS BOOK

Originally sub-titled 'The ecological [ ]
Food for a Future has been welcomed a[ ]
argument for vegetarianism and veganism. Its topicality is heightened
by mounting speculation concerning the gradual phasing-out of the
meat and dairy industries in the face of over-population, depletion
of natural resources, and a more responsible awareness of our environmental obligations. See also the Preface to this edition on page 7.

Jon Wynne-Tyson was born in 1924 and is married with two now
grown children. His previous book, *The Civilised Alternative*, was
welcomed by educationists as a study of society's values and options
(some press comments can be found on the next page). Through his
publishing firm, which he founded in 1954 after a career which included several years farming, he has made available a number of
contributions to humane thought, including Porphyry's *On Abstinence from Animal Food*, Catherine Roberts' *The Scientific Conscience*,
Manfred Kyber's *Among Animals*, Esmé Wynne-Tyson's *The Philosophy of Compassion*, the recent *Animals' Rights: a Symposium*
(edited Paterson/Ryder), and on a more domestic level Janet
Walker's *Vegetarian Cookery*.

THE CIVILISED ALTERNATIVE

'Concerned young people – and old people who are concerned about young people – will find it full of luminous good sense. A valuable book.' *The Sunday Times*

'Franciscan in its plea for humility and compassion as the great ecological virtues.' *The Ecologist*

'A controlled passion. Admirable.' *Times Literary Supplement*

'A trenchant and most heartening book, written by a man with a mind of his own who expresses both his anger and his hope with cogency and eloquence. He is strongly on the side of those of his juniors who believe there is something *radically* wrong with the modern industrial world.' Philip Toynbee, *The Observer*

'Soundly based in humanity, in good sense, and representing a good combination of what are commonly known as idealism and realism – if you define idealism as "what could happen if", and realism as "what will happen if not".' Yehudi Menuhin

'Civilised and wise.' C. P. Snow

Jon Wynne-Tyson

FOOD FOR A FUTURE

The complete case for Vegetarianism

CENTAUR PRESS

© Jon Wynne-Tyson 1975, 1976, 1979
First published by Davis-Poynter Ltd., London, 1975
Revised edition published 1976 by Sphere Books Ltd.,
London, as an Abacus paperback
Reissued 1979 with further revisions as a paperback by
Centaur Press Ltd., and in the USA in hard covers and as
a paperback by Universe Books, New York

ISBN 0 90000097 X

Set in Monotype Times

Printed in Great Britain by
Cox & Wyman Ltd, London, Reading and Fakenham

Contents

Acknowledgments

Among those for whose help and encouragement I wish to express my gratitude in these necessarily abbreviated acknowledgments are Nathaniel Altman, Dr Frey R. Ellis, Dr V. I. Furness, Christmas Humphreys, Kathleen Jannaway, Sir Arthur Knight, Leah Leneman, Dr Alan Long, Peter Roberts, Geoffrey L. Rudd, Dr E. Lester Smith, Prof. Henry Bailey Stevens, Dr Alan Stoddard, Michael Storm, Frank Avray Wilson and of course the authors and their publishers of those books and journals from which I have quoted or borrowed.

Preface to this edition

Although this book deals with the social, historical, economic, nutritional and health aspects of a more humane eating pattern, it also attempts to examine diet in the context of a philosophy for life that meets the needs of to-day. Recent events, strengthening the realisation that a humane diet must be accepted as an ecological priority, would seem to confirm that the time is ripe for such an appraisal.

As an instance of the changing climate of opinion, in late 1977 the RSPCA hosted at Trinity College, Cambridge, a two-day symposium on the ethical aspects of man's relationships with animals. The Proceedings of this symposium, which may prove to have been a landmark in the history of animal welfare, are being published early in 1979 under the title of *Animals' Rights: A Symposium.*

My own contribution to the symposium was entitled 'Dietethics: its influence on future farming patterns'. I have introduced the term 'dietethics' because I believe it to be very relevant at a time when enlightened environmentalists and laymen alike are beginning to recognise the indivisibility of violence, and to realise that our treatment of animals cannot conveniently be divorced from our treatment of each other.

On a less philosophical level, it is encouraging that in the past few years certain well-worn myths have been dispelled. The biggest, perhaps, was the belief that a vegetarian diet supplies insufficient protein. It is now acknowledged that, given enough staple food, the body is quite capable of manufacturing its own protein from an adequate supply of cereals and pulses. Even dairy products, inseparably linked to the meat industry, are admitted to be unnecessary to good health and vigorous life.

A realisation that may prove to be something of a mixed blessing is that although there are many good reasons for a reduction of our own numbers, feeding the existing or an even greater population need not be a problem. But if the habit of meat eating spreads, then population growth invites a catastrophic level of starvation. There is more than enough for us all if we adopt a dietary regime that is more natural to our physiology and hence more humane to our own and other species.

Although the demand for this book may be due to its presentation of the first complete argument for vegetarianism and veganism, it has also come at a time when in scientific, nutritional and governmental spheres it has begun to be seen that the phasing out of the meat and dairy industry is an inescapable economic and ecological necessity over the years to come. The process will doubtless be slow, but it is increasingly agreed that there is no sound nutritional, medical or social justification for ignoring the fact that pressures on world resources demand more responsible feeding patterns in the indulgent West.

By late 1978 there were further signs that the wind of change was blowing harder over the meat and dairy industry. Despite ferocious opposition from some cattle farmers, the giant Rank Hovis McDougall group was far from alone in acknowledging that such substitutes for meat as soya were here to stay and must inevitably take more of the market. In the USA the textured vegetable protein industry has for much longer been taken for granted.

With the British butter 'mountain' the highest in five years, the Centre for Agricultural Strategy, Britain's farming 'think-tank', recommended that butter be taxed, since there was 'no valid nutritional reason to justify the present subsidy.' Such pronouncements have led, as in the United States, to conflict between nutritionists and farming interests, the latter much opposed to any setting of dietary goals that might upset the status quo.

On every side, in short, the practical and expedient reasons for fundamental change are being recognised. Cost, alone, is a significant consideration at family-budget level. More importantly, animal welfare is now a political issue. In October 1978, UNESCO accepted the draft of the Universal Declaration of Animal Rights, presented with the request that the Declaration be put to the vote in the course of the next UNESCO General Assembly in 1980. The immediate aim is to secure its adoption by UNESCO first as a Resolution and later as a Convention. Ultimately it is intended that it will be put to the vote of the General Assembly of the United Nations with a view to its adoption and ratification by all of the member countries.

If, in acknowledging that the rights of animals must be protected by law against the rights of man, UNESCO has as yet placed more emphasis on obvious cruelties than on those that are more concealed by accepted habit, at least we are moving rapidly away from the time when the case for vegetarianism could be damned as an 'attack' on meat-eaters! Certainly this book is not an attempt to savage my fellow humans. Its arguments are directed at values and habits rather than at people. By that yardstick, any review of a life-style is an 'attack'. But in this case justified, I feel. A meat-eating society is, after all, constantly 'attacking' animals in an ultimate and often most barbarous manner. The animals are in dire need of spokesmen.

Jon Wynne-Tyson

Fontwell, Sussex
1979

One

A Vegetable Love

When a sentimental passion of a vegetable fashion
  must excite your languid spleen,
An attachment à la Plato for a bashful young potato
  or a not too French French bean.

W. S. Gilbert: *Patience*

EVER since man stopped being 'content with a vegetable love' there has been trouble. Even if you set little store by Adam and Eve, preferring to trace our descent from that equally uncertain era when the drought-induced savanna is suspected of having prompted our ancestors to come down out of the trees, you will have to concede that progress has not always been synonymous with improvement since some of those forebears let their natural frugivorous diet take second place to the eating of animal flesh. The trappings and technology of modern civilisation have done little to moderate the jungle values we are supposed to have left behind us.

To get the personal note out of the way, I have had a lifelong inclination to eat the kind of food that our physiological structure shows we were intended to consume. Resistant from pramhood, as are most children, to meat and cow's milk, it took only the squeals of a pig being dragged to slaughter to set my infant teeth firmly on course for a fleshless future. My mother being half inclined that way herself, my urge was given its head instead of being hammered out of me, as it is out of so many young children who instinctively resist being made to eat substances their bodies were never designed to accept.[1]

Now in middle age, with my own children having shown no signs of missing out on anything through having left meat on the animals to whom it belongs, I believe that the case for vegetarianism can and should be argued on several different levels.

But there are certain things that worry me about vegetarianism. The first is the word itself. To many, a vegetable always seems to mean a cabbage, a potato, or some other shop-weary accompaniment to whatever slice of animal or bird the housewife makes her daily main-course centrepiece. During the last few years, growing acquaintance with American, European and Eastern eating patterns has reduced intolerance towards what so many people, particularly in Britain and America, would at one time have written off immediately as a cranky diet. But vegetarians still may have to raise a tired smile when greeted by the 'Haw, haw, haw, how do you manage to stay standing on a lettuce leaf, haw, haw, haw?' of those for whom the primacy of meat is as unarguable as the coming dawn.

Yet the definition of a vegetable is clear and covers much. It means a plant, whether root, stalk, leaf, flower, fruit or seed. More narrowly, a plant cultivated for food. Almost everything we eat is derived from vegetables (plants) or from animals. The vast majority of the animals we eat are themselves vegetarian and are therefore supplying us indirectly, wastefully and at unnecessary cost with what we can consider consuming at source.

Unfortunately, the word 'vegetarian' still presents to many minds a quite inaccurate picture of the diet and beliefs of people who exclude animals (and, in the case of vegans and certain religious sects, all animal products) from their eating habits. Many, it is true, do become quite obsessed with what, when and how they eat, and extreme food faddists, whether vegetarian or not, have often given more moderate categories an undeserved reputation. This has long been one of the social hazards of subscribing to unorthodox ideas. Health and food addicts, however, should not be confused with the ethic, nor necessarily with the practice, of vegetarianism. In the wide world of food reform there are certainly many vegetarians to be found, but numerous food reformers are no nearer to vegetarianism than a Masai tribesman or any other staunch supporter of the meat-with-or-without-two-veg school.

At this point a further definition is called for. Identifying a vegetarian as someone who avoids eating flesh of any kind (meat, fowl or fish), the fourteenth (1973) edition of the *Encyclopaedia Britannica* states that 'most vegetarians use milk and milk products; those in the modern Occident usually eat eggs also, but most vegetarians in India exclude them, as did those in the classical Mediterranean lands. Vegetarians who exclude animal products altogether have taken the name vegans, and those who use milk and milk products are sometimes called lacto-vegetarians.' This definition is the one accepted by both British and American vegetarian societies. The word 'vegetarian' was coined in 1842 from the Latin 'vegetus' (whole, sound, fresh, lively) and should not be confused with a 'vegetable-arian' (a mythical human whom some imagine subsisting entirely on vegetables in the limited, colloquial sense of that word – that is, on plant life that for some mysterious reasons excludes even such naturals as nuts, fruit, grains, etc.).

In everyday usage, 'vegetarian' tends to mean someone who cuts meat out of his diet but probably eats eggs and dairy products. 'Lacto-vegetarian' or even 'lacto-ovo-vegetarian' are more exact terms for those who exclude animal flesh but eat everything else, but they are normally used only where precise distinctions are called for. A 'vegan', however, is in a quite definite category. He is concerned to eat only plant life, and in some cases excludes even honey. In this book I have at times used 'vegetarian' where 'lacto-' or 'lacto-ovo-vegetarian' would have been more accurate, and on other occasions have used it generically to include vegans. The context should prevent confusion. But where veganism is mentioned it means only one thing – the exclusion of all animal products.

The second thing that worries me about vegetarianism is far more fundamental and important than any definition, and this is the very fact that it has become an 'ism'. The world is riddled with -isms and -ologies and -anities; with specialists and experts; with divisions, categories and compartmental thinking; and so with barriers, suspicions, ignorance, antagonisms, jealousies, strife, cruelty, wars and a sad array of stupidity and suffering. Although this is not the place to pursue the matter in depth,[2] I believe that if there is one -ism worth hanging on to, it is eclecticism – the method of selecting from various systems such opinions, facts and values as are judged to be sound. Those who resist the restrictions and confusions imposed by 'labels', preferring to seek the elements of truth that are to be found in many systems, and to create therefrom a philosophy that is both subjectively satisfying and points towards a more workable social pattern, are likely to adopt a more natural and compassionate diet simply because this would be a logical step in the formulation of a consistent life-style. It 'fits'. This is why I suggest that vegetarianism should not be studied or adopted in isolation, but should be seen as part of a way (a more eclectic and eco-*logical* way) of life that may help our species to attain a higher level of physical and mental health than we have known before.

Even leaving aside any importance that may be placed on forming a personal philosophy, there can be no denying that food monopolises a large part of our lives. Whether we think it a crashing bore deserving as little time and thought as possible, or whether we pride ourselves on being gourmets, we all have to spend a lot of time thinking about the stuff; growing, buying, preparing, consuming it; and washing up after it.

Anything that affects so deeply our physical and mental environment cannot be left to chance and mere preference. Little that we do affects us more than the nature of the substances we eat and drink – not only in terms of man-hours but especially in relation to our psycho-physical equilibrium. It says in the *Dhammapada*, the most famous scripture of the Buddhist canon, 'All that we are is the result of what we have thought.' It has been said more recently that we are what we eat.

Apart from not taking the rôle food plays in our lives for granted, economic and ecological facts make it increasingly necessary to consider all the grounds for choosing what and how much we eat. On this score at least there can be little disagreement among dieticians, doctors, food reformers, vegetarians, farmers, demographers, environmentalists, and anyone else

11

concerned with our eating habits and their effect on our lives and surroundings.

As will be suggested later, there are other reasons why we should be prepared to question these habits, and I am well aware that much that has to be said may strike an unresponsive chord in a good many hearts. Nearly all of us dislike breaking with custom. But in the sense of having more facts at our finger tips, we are today potentially better educated than in any other period of history, and this new era of knowledge has brought with it responsibilities we cannot ignore. The problems of over-population, pollution and man's place in the scheme of things compel reassessments in many spheres. Our habits of eating have also to be questioned. Mankind has reached many crossroads in a relatively short history. The one we happen to be at at the moment is sign-posted to the need to question practices which might not have called for general scrutiny unless the over-abundance of our species had not brought home to us that the world is finite; our greed and short-sightedness have already done such damage to our environment, and have now so depleted the earth's resources, that we are in very real danger of self-annihilation.

So this book is not concerned solely with whether soya beans have more protein than beef, with the evidence for one kind of food being better for our health than another, with the moral considerations that should arise from our daily inhumanity to millions of sentient creatures. It is concerned with all these things and many others, but at the same time it attempts to suggest some kind of synthesis: to show that not only do we owe it to ourselves to examine our eating habits, but also to our environment, to the species with whom we share that environment, and perhaps above all to our children and those future generations whose very existence will be determined by the path we choose to take today. We are beginning to realise that there is a moral order within the newly rediscovered science of ecology. It is an order that must take account of the future as much as of the present.

I hope that this book will also lead to the discovery that a diet that excludes the meat of animals can be enjoyable, simpler, more healthy, and undoubtedly less expensive than orthodox eating patterns. Since the economic pressures in our over-peopled world are anyway going to make the popularisation of meat-substitutes inevitable, the sooner we realise that necessity carries positive benefits, the better.

Before going any further I would like to clarify what I mean by two of the words chosen for the sub-title of this book – 'The ecological priority of a humane diet'.

Most of us think of 'diet' as meaning food that has been prescribed in certain quantities or of a certain kind. But in the past it had a far wider meaning, and a much better one. It stood for 'A way of living or thinking'. While its present-day use is perfectly appropriate for this book, I believe the arguments I put forward will be better understood for bearing in mind the broader definition.

'Ecological' deserves even closer examination. Ecology, that 'branch of biology which deals with the natural relations between organisms and their environment', or if one takes the sociological definition, 'the study of the spatial distribution of a population in reference to material and social causes and effects' (SOED), is more than a useful and topical word. It stands for a concept of life and values in which the practical, the ethical and the philosophical elements are (or should be) given equal weight. Employed in this, its most mature, sense, it goes a long way towards standing for that compound of wonder, knowledge, faith and fierce inner need for a sense of direction and framework of behaviour that first prompted the notion of a supreme God.

As with the word 'diet', the 'ecological' of my sub-title may be used in either the narrow or broader sense. I hope that as the argument of the book is developed the reader may move nearer to accepting the wider interpretation. I believe that our growing concept of ecology is prompting a vision that could be said to be nothing less than a modern yet essentially eternal philosophy for contemporary and future existence. A vision that may destroy *di*vision, perhaps helping to build that much-needed bridge between science and those less material concerns that provide the main evidence that mankind is (or at least can become) more than a race of merely clever apes. It is a vision that, although so badly needed, has been pushed aside rather than never before examined. It was Victor Hugo who wrote:

It was first of all necessary to civilise man in relation to his fellow men. That task is already well-advanced and makes progress daily. But it is also necessary to civilise man in relation to nature. There, everything remains to be done ... Philosophy has concerned itself but little with man beyond man, and has examined only superficially, almost with a smile of disdain, man's relationship with things, and with animals, which in his eyes are merely things. But are there not depths here for the thinker? Must one suppose oneself mad because one has the sentiment of universal pity in one's heart? Are there not certain laws of mysterious equity that pertain to the whole sum of things, and that are transgressed by the thoughtless, useless behaviour of man to animals? ... For myself I believe that pity is a law like justice, and that kindness is a duty like uprightness. That which is weak has the right to the kindness and pity of that which is strong. Animals are weak because they are less intelligent. Let us therefore be kind and compassionate towards them. In the relations of man with the animals, with the flowers, with all the objects of creation, there is a whole great ethic [*toute une grande morale*] scarcely seen as yet, but which will eventually break through into the light and be the corollary and the complement to human ethics.

Two

The Social Obligation

If man has gained his intellectual dominance over his fellow creatures by concentrating his evolutionary energies on the development of his brain, it remains to be seen whether h? can now maintain his position by contriving a method of living in orderly relations with members of his own species. If he fails to do so, he may yet follow the example of many other groups of animals who have achieved a temporary ascendancy by exaggerated development of some particular structural mechanism. He may become extinct.

Professor W. E. le Gros Clark, FRS, in
History of the Primates

The predatory life ... brings little progress in social organisation ... Predaceous man unlike other forms of predatory life preys on its own species. With predaceous man civilisation itself becomes of predatory type ... Economic warfare, commercial warfare, class-warfare, are symptomatic of homo praedatorius. *He exploits cruelty on sub-human lives as well as on human life ... Man's altruism has to grow. It is not enough for him to stand and deplore. That is less to mend things than to run from them. A positive charity is wanted; negation is not enough. In effect it needs a self-growth, which shall open out a finer self. It requires to absorb in 'feeling' something of the world beyond the self and put it alongside the interests of the very self ... A great gift - some might say divine - comes to the 'self' when perceiving certain suffering external to itself it so reacts to it that suffering becomes its own, and is shared even as a 'feeling' ... Altruism as passion ... nature's noblest product; the greatest contribution made by man to life.*

Sir Charles Sherrington, OM, GBE, FRS, MA, MD,
DSc (Cantab), FRCP, FRCS, in *Man on his Nature*

ALTHOUGH the various 'orthodox' arguments for a vegetarian diet are as relevant as they ever were, the rapid expansion of the industrial societies has created a case for the decline of meat-eating that is compelling.

No one reading a newspaper needs to be told of the problems that we have brought upon ourselves by the spread of our species. The 'infestation of humanity', as one writer has put it, means quite simply that it is becoming increasingly irresponsible to eat meat. Even if we do not care about the aesthetics and health dangers, or about the needless sufferings of the hun-

15

dreds of millions of creatures we slaughter every year, we cannot ignore any longer the fact that eating flesh is a wantonly selfish and short-sighted practice.

This aspect will be considered in greater depth later, but think for a moment what the habit of meat-eating involves in terms of the world's food supplies. It means the extensive growing of crops, notably grain, in order to feed them to animals from which, after an expensive interval, we take back in exchange an absurdly disproportionate quantity of food in a form that we hallow, quite incorrectly, as being far superior to the plant-life from which it was derived. In addition to being fed the corn that requires great tracts of the world's land supply, the animals themselves, even in these days of 'factory-farming', still need further huge areas for pasture.

About four-fifths of the world's agricultural land is used for feeding animals, and only about one-fifth for feeding man directly. This fact, shocking in its implications, has been examined by nutritionists Frank Wokes (editor-in-chief of *Plant Foods for Human Nutrition* and chairman of the Plant Foods Research Trust) and Cyril Vesey (University Department of Clinical Neurology, London) in their paper 'Land, Food and the People', Part One of the series *Perspectives in Nutrition*:

At the beginning of this decade there were about 35 hundred million people in the world ... The rich Western nations occupying about half of the world's agricultural land amounted to only about two-sevenths of the world's population; whereas the poor, mainly Eastern, occupying the other half of the world's agricultural land, amounted to about five-sevenths. Moreover, the poor Eastern people live mainly in the tropics where the yields of crops are often less than a quarter of those in the Western countries. Multiplying the yields factor of about 4 by the population density factor of about $2\frac{1}{2}$, we get a differential of about 10 between the average food crop production of the average Westerner and that of the average Easterner. The average Westerner does not, of course, eat 10 times but only about $1\frac{1}{2}$ times as much food as the average Easterner. But he consumes much more animal food, about five times as much animal protein and animal calories as the average Easterner. He is able to do this only because he has two-and-a-half times as much agricultural land on which to produce his food, and this on the average is several times more fertile. But because the people in Western countries consume much more animal food, he even needs to import food materials to feed his animals as well as himself.

To sum up the world food position: we have two-sevenths of richer people, more spread out, and eating more animal food, in contrast to five-sevenths of poorer people crowded together and eating much less animal food in proportion to plant food.

It should be added that this grossly inequitable situation is being worsened by the advent of factory-farming which is producing a population explosion of animals as providers of human food that is outstripping the human population explosion in a galloping competition for the basic plant foods.

When we consider the work and cost and wastage that goes into stock-breeding in order that the world's affluent minority can indulge so unnecessary a luxury, the sheer extravagance and foolishness of it all is staggering. We read in our newspapers about the starving and under-fed millions, and all the time we are feeding to meat-producing animals the very crops that could more than eradicate world food shortage; also, we are importing from starving nations large quantities of grain and other foods that are then fed to our animals instead of to the populations who produced them.

No one need be surprised by the reference to the affluent *minority's* habit of meat-eating. Were flesh-eating human beings not a minority group, the present world-population would be far smaller than it is (perhaps the only argument that could be made out in favour of eating meat!). With cattle needing many times more land for food and rearing than do people, and returning to us such a small proportion of the food they eat, our planet has already got more than its economic quota of omnivorous humans.

If this extremely uneconomic way of obtaining food had been adopted by all nations, the land resources of the world would long ago have been exhausted. Most of the fertile land devoted to cattle – which eat cereals, root and green crops and various seeds for improved milk production – could show a much quicker and more economical return if used for crops suitable for direct feeding to human beings. Animals eat 20 pounds of protein for every pound they yield as meat. In comparing plant with animal food production in terms of yields per acre in less developed and more developed countries it has been shown that

the plant protein production from cereals and pulses was three to six times the production of milk protein from the same area under the same conditions. For plant protein from leafy vegetables it was seven to twelve times. When these plant/animal ratios were measured against meat protein they were approximately doubled. On the average about a fifth of the plant protein fed to animals becomes available for human consumption as milk, and about a tenth of it is turned into meat. These approximate fifth and tenth figures which take into consideration the amount of protein needed to rear the animal to the age when it will produce milk, and to maintain it between the different lactation periods, summarised the findings of experts in different countries and in our opinion gave a fair picture of the plant/animal position in terms of protein production. A similar picture was obtained from comparison of the relative consumption of plant protein with that of animal protein in human diets in different countries. In China, India and other countries in the Far East containing about half the world's population, the plant/animal ratios for dietary protein range from six to eight. Only in Western Europe does the average consumption of animal protein become about equal to that of plant protein, and in the USA somewhat exceeds it. (Editorial, *Plant Foods for Human Nutrition*, Vol. 1. No. 2, February 1969, Pergamon Press).

The conclusion to these findings suggested that plant protein would play an increasingly important part in solving the world food problem, and in the few years since those words their prediction has been echoed many times.

It is to our shame that such revelations are far from new. Much further back Sir John Russell, FRS, and others before him, made similar estimates showing incontrovertibly that plant foods, if fed directly to man rather than after processing through animals, can increase the yield per acre by up to ten fold. As an example, soya beans yield seven times as much amino-acid per acre as milk production and eight times as much as egg production. Animals are incapable of yielding more protein and energy per acre than the plants they themselves consume. 'Plant foods (fed directly to man) can result in a much more efficient use of land . . . Production of a whole new range of processed plant foods such as texturised vegetable protein (TVP), soya and other vegetable milks, and protein from micro-organisms (SCP), is steadily increasing.' (Leader, *Plant Foods for Man*, Vol. 1, No. 1, Autumn 1973, Newman).

Plant foods create protein from water, carbon dioxide and nitrogen, which is why they are the primary source of protein in the world today. But animals have to eat the plants, or eat other animals, to get their protein. The cow can convert poor protein and other nitrogenous compounds into protein of a better quality, but it is an extremely inefficient and wasteful machine for so doing. At huge expense it consumes a large amount of plant food and converts it into a small quantity of meat. This above all is why governments, economists, industrialists and international welfare organisations have begun to realise that the sooner the cow, the chicken and other victims of our prodigal way of life are replaced by food made from plant proteins (or even – novel idea – by the plant themselves), the better for the world at large. Mixed vegetable proteins can be as good as, and far better than, meat. When that fact is not only fully realised, but universally acted upon, books like this will be unnecessary.[1]

It is not that we have not known these facts, but rather that we have not wished to face their implications. This would have meant recognising a moral and economic obligation to sacrifice cherished habits, and the rest of the world can rot before most of us will do that. It is relevant at this point to include the following tables which are based on figures given in *Indian Agriculture in Brief* (*1966*) (Directorate of Economics and Statistics, Ministry of Food, Agriculture Community Development and Co-operation, Government of India).

It will be seen from the second table that fruits and vegetables need to be taken in greater bulk, but they compare well with other foods as sources of different nutrients if their moisture content is taken into account. Their dry weight is only about a fifth of fresh weight. Leafy vegetables are concentrated sources of calcium, iron and carotene, even on the basis of fresh weight.[2]

These facts and figures comprise only a fraction of the evidence for the vital importance of plant foods in solving the problems of India and other malnourished countries. Compared with milk and meat, plant foods are cheaper sources with 5–10 times the yield of calories, proteins and other essential nutrients. High yields of some nutrients claimed for intensive milk production in the UK are not applicable to those encountered in India. Biological values of staple plant proteins may be made comparable with those of animal proteins by blending different plant proteins and by fortifying them with lysine and with vitamin B12. In India the proportion of the cereal crops that is diverted to animal feeding is less than a tenth of that so diverted in the UK, but much groundnut protein, left in the residue from peanut oil production, is wasted by feeding to animals or even by being used as manure.

As a single instance of the folly of what is going on, each year we take from India, a land with so long an experience of famine, many thousands of tons of oilseed protein to feed battery farm animals. Yet an ounce of protein a day could make all the difference between life and death to a starving child. A thought that presumably does not unduly worry those who insist upon eating meat.[3]

If in having a social conscience we are not merely working through a current fashion that will before long be as obsolete as bee-hive hair-dos or bustles, what should we be expecting of ourselves in an age when the abundance of information available gives us no excuse for ignorance and inactivity? In the past, the hypocrisy of those who chose limited rôles for their indignation and social conscience was largely innocent. They simply did not have the facts necessary to relate cause to effect, or to see the total picture.

Today's situation is quite different. We are fed information from all directions. Unlike our computers, however, our storage systems are grossly inefficient. The effectiveness of our memory banks is determined not by the total number of facts we take in, but by the number we wish to reject. We select our facts dishonestly, and as a consequence develop a totally unbalanced 'memory' that makes our actions stupid, and our reactions inconsistent, anti-social, and ultimately self-destructive. We cannot see the whole because we are so busy trying to preserve and defend the part that suits our personal inclinations and weaknesses.

With around 20,000,000 starving people and many times that number seriously malnourished, on (or off) our consciences today, the richer minority which preserves the unnecessary and wasteful habit of consuming dead animals is having it brought home that the only *eco*-logical next step is to stop eating meat and other animal products. For as we continue to destroy the life-support systems of our planet, the graph of starvation and

Table 1. Relative efficiency of vegetable foods and animal foods as suppliers of nutrients from an acre of land

Foodstuffs	Gross yield per acre (kg)	Approximate amount available per acre*					
		Calories $\times 10^5$	Protein (kg)	Calcium (kg)	Iron (g)	Vitamin A $\times 10^5$	Riboflavin (kg)
Cereals	350	12·0	35	0·10	21·0	3·5	0·35
Pulses	250	8·6	60	0·20	20·0	5·5	0·75
Oilseeds	300	16·5	78	0·15	4·8	1·8	0·90
Milk	360	2·4	12	0·63	0·6	3·0	0·30
Animal foods	20	0·4	4	0·05	0·4	0·1	0·06
Leafy vegetables	5000–10000	24–48	200–400	125–250	750–1500	3500–7000	5–10
Root vegetables	5000–10000	50–100	100–200	10–20	30–60	50–100	5–10
Other vegetables	2500–5000	10–20	50–100	1–2	50–100	75–150	1·5–3·0
Fruits	10000–20000	50–100	80–160	3–6	120–140	50–100	2–4
Sugar	2000	80					

* Calculated from figures for yield and average nutrient composition of different food groups derived from values given in food tables for commonly consumed foods.

Table 2. Different foodstuffs as sources of selected nutrients

Foodstuffs	Approximate amount (g) giving					
	100 cal	10 g protein	100 mg calcium	3 mg iron	1000 i.u. vitamin A	1 mg riboflavin
Cereals	30	100	330	50	1000	1000
Pulses	30	40	125	40	1000	250
Oilseeds	20	40	200	200	600	330
Milk	125	300	50	1500	1000	1000
Animal foods	70	40	400	150	3300	330
Egg	60	75	170	150	50	500
Leafy vegetables	200	250	40	20	15	1000
Starchy root vegetables	100	500	500	500	1000	5000
Other vegetables	250	500	250	150	330	1700
Fruits	(a) 100 (b) 200	1200	300	250	(c) 100 (d) 2000	5000

(a) and (b) Fruits low and high in carbohydrate.
(c) and (d) Fruits poor and rich in carotene.

shortage can only rise, however sheltered from such facts we may be by the media and our own wishful thinking. In our greed to profit from the under-developed world, we have already gone to great lengths to popularise meat-eating among nations whose diet was previously largely or wholly meat-excluding. As world income levels have risen, the demand for meat has increased, causing the expanding livestock industries to compete for grain crops as a source of animal feed. Having sold the underprivileged nations the ugly notion that a steak a day is the status goal to aim for, we are now beginning to realise that our campaigns will prove to be self-defeating. We are encouraging other countries to compete for the very resources of which we are already running short ourselves. A-political though the arguments for a meatless diet are and must remain, there can be few more graphic examples than that of the short-sightedness of capitalist economics.

But such is the nature of the 'beast', that alongside these efforts to popu-larise a habit that more than any other needs abandoning, the industrial West is already researching into and producing alternatives that may mark the beginning of a climate of thought that will lead to phasing out the breeding and butchery on which so many of us rely for our daily dinners. Although a fair amount of publicity has been given to this fact in connec-tion with the under-developed nations (see page 17 above), so powerful are the mechanisms by which the bulk of meat-eaters exclude from their recognition any news which might affect their habits that few read or under-stood the signs. Yet the manufacture of meat analogues for the Western nations is already a sizable industry, especially in the USA. In Europe the use of vegetable proteins, whether 'textured' or not, is less taken for granted than in North America, but is already established to a greater ex-tent than the man in the street (or even the woman in the supermarket, unless she takes the trouble to read the writing on the packets) realises.

It is an unfortunate fact of modern life that the right things all too often happen for the wrong reasons. The gradual replacement of meat by vege-table proteins has almost nothing to do with any general concern for the sufferings of animals, nor even with the welfare or aesthetic sensitivity of humans. The impulse to explore and develop the market may have come in part from observance of starvation and malnutrition levels, but far and away the greatest spur has been good old-fashioned greed. Quite simply, eating meat is a very expensive habit all along the line. It costs more to produce and more to buy than any other staple part of our diet, so much so that at the time of writing many families are already down to one meat meal a week for the unpraiseworthy but significant reason that they cannot afford more.

With the arrival of meat analogues, however, palatable and nutritious protein is becoming available to anyone at a cost that is below that of many standard items of our diet – and certainly well below the cost of meat. What is more, there is every reason to suppose that analogues, some of which are already virtually indistinguishable from the real thing, will before long be available at prices comparable to some of the least expensive items on the housewife's shopping list – such as beans and peas, for instance, for that is what many of the analogues are made of. The process of converting vegetables into protein without employing the intermediary of a living animal is, or as demand grows will be, in all essentials extremely simple and inexpensive (Appendix II is a brief statement on the economics of man-made fibres in the field of nutrition). Quite a lot of the present cost lies in the research necessary to produce the texture and flavour of dead animals – a concern at which future generations may well look back with amused incredulity, for there can be little doubt that once the acceptance of vegetable proteins is widespread, a variety of textures and flavours will become available and may in time largely or entirely replace those really very limited meat flavours which today so many of us, through sheer custom, value so highly.

However, new food sources, whether of textured or direct plant form, must fit into the accepted dietary patterns of developing countries. Food scientists in Illinois have recently been concentrating on developing simple ways of preparing whole soya beans, using equipment which can be found in any village. They have found easy ways of preventing the slightly unpleasant flavour of cooked soya beans from developing, and have also produced a range of dry flaky foods to which other natural ingredients can be added for flavour. Such flakes and flours can be used to prepare traditional breads, chapatis, tortillas and so forth in conjunction with local cereals. A prototype baby-weaning food and a milky beverage are already proving very successful in India.

In his paper 'More Protein from Field and Factory', W. F. J. Cuthbertson of Glaxo Research Limited has written:

There is in fact now a possibility not only of banishing hunger and malnutrition from the world, but also of reducing much expensive and disagreeable farm work such as the rearing and slaughter of animals . . . In the production of meat analogues most of the original protein becomes available for human consumption . . . Protein cannot be fully utilised without sufficient calories. In populations existing at the borderline between hunger and starvation, the children often receive protein in quantities which would be adequate if they took enough calories, i.e. total food of all types. Because they do not have that food they manifest signs of protein deficiency. This 'induced' protein-calorie deficiency can often be abolished rapidly if enough extra food can be given to prevent hunger. In such circumstances the protein content of this extra food may be of small consequence. In the development of food crops most emphasis has been placed on the production of cereals – rice, wheat and maize – because these constitute the staple food of many people and supply a large proportion of the protein and calories that they require. Indeed, if enough cereal is provided to a population to prevent hunger, then that diet will also supply enough protein for all except the young children . . . The protein in meat analogues can be of high biological value, equivalent to that of meat . . . there is also a bonus benefit, compared with meat, of low cholesterol levels . . . The fact that the basic protein-aceous materials for structured proteins are closely standardised chemically and physically helps the manufacturer to produce food items with uniform characteristics. A further advantage to both manufacturer and user is the fact that in preparing structured foods there is no risk of contamination with bone, cartilage, fur, feathers or excreta; moreover the absence of bone, fat and skin in the final products makes their use simpler and eliminates waste. Because of the useful characteristics of these new protein foods their consumption is increasing rapidly. In 1966 sales were about $1 million in the USA, but by 1969 had passed the $10 million mark. A growth of sales of some hundredfold is expected by 1980. (*World Health*, November 1971.)

But welcome though such recognition of plant values may be, we should keep the facts in perspective. As Magnus Pyke has remarked: 'When people hear of artificial meat, they usually think the important thing is that science is helping to feed the world's starving millions. Not so! Knitted steak made out of soya-bean protein, peanuts or haricot beans does not add anything to the food supply. The people who eat the artificial would get as much nourishment or more if they ate the beans or the peanuts in the first place.' (*Sunday Mirror*, 22.10.1972.)

In essence, this is true enough, though the slightly derogatory 'knitted steak' dig is rather unscientific. Soya flour can be compared with wheat flour, and just as bread is a textured form of wheat flour, so textured vegetable protein is a similar form of soya flour. The chief rôle of the analogues, perhaps, is to bring us back to square one – to help the transition from animal to plant food via substances that taste of the one but are derived from the other. Alex Comfort's statement that 'with the Third World short of protein, it is inevitable that beef – which is as wasteful in production as grouse, and comes from pathologically fat-loaded beasts – will have to give place to textured vegetable protein' (*Guardian*, 8.2.1973) was, indeed, a statement of inevitability rather than necessity. If we refuse to do the sensible thing the sensible way (that it, by the exercise of our reason), then we have to be tempted like small children. The way things are going, what matters most is just how quickly we can be persuaded to fall into temptation.

Linked with what we are beginning to see to be our social obligation to phase out the eating of meat and animal products is our new-found awareness of man's folly in having ignored the ecological facts of life. As we have been learning fast in recent years, all nature is, or strives to be, in a state of balance. That balance is essential for the well-being of all. Sporadic natural cataclysms apart, the physical world achieves and retains a workable balance except when man, whose inquisitive intelligence far outstrips his intellectual wisdom, attempts to fight against or outsmart nature. Then and only then do the real troubles begin.

Man's interference with the natural world has of course extended far beyond his eating habits. No one today needs reminders of the many ways in which men have tampered with the environment, usually for short-term gain at the cost of long-term damage. If we can accept the Buddhist concept of *karma* we might well judge that the mess we have made of our world is the direct outcome of our irresponsible and greed-provoked actions. If the only release from *karma* is to be obtained by knowledge and abstinence, as the Buddhists and most great philosophies have taught, then the remedy is obvious and precisely accords with what in the West we term ecological awareness. We must develop a better sense of responsibility towards our total environment. However reluctant the diehards among us may be to admit it, this better sense cannot any longer exclude from revision the staples of our diet.

Quite clearly the eating of meat is not going to cease over-night, and many would argue that our social obligations should not permit too abrupt an alteration of the *status quo*. They need not worry. None of the hysterical paraphernalia that greets sudden change need be provoked by the facts we have to face. No columns of placard-bearing farmers and butchers need be seen winding through Times Square or down Whitehall. The changes that have to come will doubtless continue to be gradual, though perhaps far from imperceptible to this generation.

It is nevertheless important that we no longer withhold from ourselves and from those who are younger the philosophy, or the ecological ethic, that lies behind the necessity. For although the changeover may not be dramatic, the sooner it comes the better for those who have for so long suffered from our addiction to animal protein. Not a day passes but that the world's environment is damaged both obviously and subtly by the demands we make upon it. We are part of that environment, and cannot escape the consequences of our irresponsibility, however much faith we may place in the ingenuity of tomorrow and in those scientists and technologists who attempt to persuade us that anything nature does man can do better.

Notes

1. The relationship between meat and milk production is close and intricate. The problems of the dairy industry are greatly increased not only by production levels that depend on trends in breeding herds, the importing and exporting of live animals, and marketing patterns, but by the high cost of feeding stuffs. With dairy farming now supplying over 80 per cent of all calves for the veal and beef trade, the inter-relationship of the two facets of the industry becomes clearer. The

Sunday joint recently nearly doubled in cost in about one year, milk threatening to follow suit unless farmers could keep down the level of their compound feeding, so reducing the availability of meat and provoking even higher prices. (Over 600 British farms abandoned milk production in July 1975 alone, and the national herd was being slaughtered at the rate of 100,000 a year.) Either way, animal products are likely to rise to even dizzier heights while greedy nations insist on getting their protein second-hand through herds of inefficient four-legged machines whose rôle in the economy no conscientious time-and-motion man could possibly defend.

2. For amplification of this argument, which is particularly relevant to deficient diets in undeveloped countries, the reader is referred to the paper 'Horticulture in Relation to Nutritional Requirements' by R. Rajalakshmi and C. V. Ramakrishnan, Department of Biochemistry, MS University, Baroda, India, and to other papers published in *Plant Foods for Human Nutrition* (Vol. 1, No. 2, February 1969, Pergamon Press), a journal of great importance in the nutritional field.

3. In a paper discussing leaf and microbial protein sources, and arguing that the rapid expansion of the yield of food supplies of vegetable origin is essential to beating malnutrition, A. N. Kurtha, MSc, has written ('Potential Supplies of Foods of Vegetable Origin'):

Oilseed meals are at present used mainly in cattle feed and fertiliser. If these were upgraded to human foods, large quantities of proteins would become immediately available to combat dietary deficiencies of protein (Parpa, 1968). These oilseed meals are the dry protein-rich residue left after the vegetable oil has been extracted from the plant material such as soya beans, peanut, cotton-seed and sunflower seed. However, oilseed-meal protein is deficient in certain essential amino acids and therefore has to be used in collaboration with, for instance, legumes or synthetic amino acids to confer a balanced amino acid content. Such mixed foods then have a high nutritive value and are considerably cheaper than conventional high protein foods. Oilseed meals have a protein content of 40–50 per cent, but most traditional methods for the preparation of these do not result in products fit for human consumption. However, it is possible today to produce good quality edible protein from soya beans, coconut, sesame, peanuts and sunflower seeds. After soya bean protein, groundnuts are the largest source of oilseed protein in the world. Groundnuts are deficient in methionine and lysine, but if used in conjunction with lysine-rich legumes the quality of the protein is markedly improved. A number of products based on oilseed meals have been developed in Asia, South America and Africa. For example, the Institute of Central America and Panama (INCAP) developed a very popular protein-rich mixture called Mixture 9B. It consists of 38 per cent cotton-seed flour, 29 per cent sorghum, 29 per cent maize, 3 per cent Torula yeast, vitamins and minerals. In India a product called Indian Multipurpose Food Supplement (IMFS) was produced, which consisted of 75 per cent edible grade peanut flour, 21 per cent chickpea flour, vitamins and minerals. This has a protein content of 42 per cent.

Groundnut protein is the most important constituent of Indian famine relief foods. In 1970 Britain imported from India groundnut meal the equivalent of a year's ration for 13,000,000 children, expressly to feed animals. In 1973 some 150,000 tons of oilseed protein were imported. Government spokesmen have suggested that much of it would be destroyed by pests or damp if it were not imported, but a genuine foreign aid programme should include know-how and equipment to enable hungry countries to help themselves.

26

Three

The Aberrant Ape

Apes and men were fundamentally vegetarian, just as otters and ferrets were fundamentally flesh-eaters.

Sir Peter Chalmers Mitchell, late Secretary of the Zoological Society of London

The apes and monkeys, which man nearly resembles in his dentition, derive their staple food from fruits, grain, the kernels of nuts, and other forms in which the most sapid and nutritious tissues of the vegetable kingdom are elaborated; and the close resemblance . . . shows that man was, from the beginning, adapted to eat the fruit of the trees of the garden.

Professor Sir Richard Owen, FRS

Fruits, roots and the succulent parts of vegetables appear to be the natural food of man: his hands afford him a facility in gathering them; and his short and comparatively weak jaws, his short canine teeth not passing beyond the common line of the others, and the tubercular teeth, would not permit him either to feed on herbage or devour flesh, unless those aliments were previously prepared by the culinary processes.

Baron Cuvier

Man by nature was never made to be a carnivorous animal, nor is he armed for prey or rapine, with jagged and pointed teeth, and claws to rend and tear; but with gentle hands to gather fruit and vegetables, and with teeth to chew and eat them.

John Ray, FRS

NOT everyone is concerned about his social obligations. Many of us are occupied with extracting from life the maximum gain for the minimum cost. If principle is involved, it is increasingly likely to be the pleasure principle. To the hedonist a social conscience is strictly for the next man down the line.

Very well, then that is how things are. But so far from this providing the pleasure-chaser with a reason for ignoring the argument of this book, he more than most needs to focus his attention on one aspect in particular. Although development of a social conscience posits long-term considerations that your 'What's-in-it-for-me?' character may feel he can afford to ignore, there is one short-term need that no thorough-going hedonist can do without, and that is good health.

In every organism good health depends upon observance of certain rules. In recent years this fact has been made increasingly obvious to students of the environment. The science of ecology has prompted a now rapidly spreading awareness of the fact that natural laws cannot be successfully flouted. Something has to give.

One of the most obvious facts that a more broadly based study of the world has made clear is that every animal is adapted to take a special kind of food. Feed a tiger on lettuce and you get a sick tiger. Feed a pony on slices of ham and the knacker will be in business.

The right food means life. The wrong food can mean anything from diminished physical and mental activity to disease and even death. If anyone seriously doubts that statement he might as well return this book to its shelf and either take out a hunk of escapist fiction or steep himself in some basic texts. The graveyards are full of wishful thinkers.

The importance of food in our lives is not, of course, confined to the arguments for or against a flesh diet. There is no lack of books on nutrition, a great many of which emphasise our growing realisation that the processes by which so-called civilised man 'improves' his food are in need of urgent review. Every day more evidence is produced to strengthen the case against the refining, preserving, dyeing and general tampering that goes on with almost everything we eat.

But mere food-centred health-faddism can be something of a yawn. If not careful, it is easy to become so concerned about the purity of our food that the sheer worry of it all may have as bad an effect upon our health as eating the stuff we are trying to avoid. There must be balance in everything. There is, nevertheless, much evidence that a technology harnessed to the bandwagon of economic growth (that is, to profits) is responsible for devitalising so much of what we eat every day of our lives. There is no doubt about this. What each one of us has to face is just how far, individually, we are prepared to travel on the bandwagon.

When one reads physiologists' and nutritionists' evidence of the many diseases that are due to wrong food, and of how important for our health the right food is, it may seem difficult to understand why the medical profession has not spoken out more strongly. Some might say it would be naïve to expect doctors to encourage the prevention of those diseases by which they earn their livings. But that would be a cynical judgment. A fairer and nearer explanation is that doctors, no less than anyone else, are creatures of habit, brainwashed by the traditions of their calling (not to mention the drug houses) just as much as by the behavioural patterns we all share.

It must still be said, however, that orthodox medicine deserves only our

28

qualified approval until it is prepared to place far more importance on the connection between what we eat and how we are. It is grossly unscientific, indeed truly 'cranky', to ignore man's physiological structure and then attempt to treat the ills he brings upon himself by remedies often as unnatural and suspect as the practices that have caused the disease in the first place.

Such thinking has produced the obscenity of those laboratories in which enormous numbers of animals are subjected to often painful and sometimes barbaric experiments set up, with unsurprisingly small success, to find cures for the ills resulting from those non-instinctual habits men have invented and refuse to give up. If we choose to over-indulge our bodies, to pollute and ravish our environment, and to cultivate habits that mere commonsense should tell us are inadvisable if not suicidal, it is monstrous that we should add to our crimes against ourselves a list of far less excusable cruelties and abuses towards species innocent of responsibility for our self-induced problems.

This is not a digression. In a society where the general practitioner is usually our only guide to better health, it is vital that we understand just how far to trust orthodox medicine to know what is best for us. Too many doctors still lag way behind the knowledge that is available to them. It is hardly surprising that medical science shows such faith in drug prescriptions when one sees how slow so many practitioners are to admit that prevention is preferable to attempted cure. On the other hand, what a task they are faced with in educating most of us to take a blind bit of notice of any warning that might interfere with what we want to do or eat! We cannot blame doctors disproportionately for our own lazy-mindedness and self-indulgence.

The case against such abuses to our physiology as refined flour and sugar (*Pure, White and Deadly* as John Yudkin called his recent book), excessive alcohol and so on, is clear and in all essentials proven. But it differs from the case against flesh eating in one important respect. Where refined flour and sugar are concerned, the original ingredient can at least be said to bear some relation to man's physiological requirements. They are plant foods. What the chemists and technologists may do to make them more deceptively palatable, or cheaper, or prettier, or bulkier, or longer-lasting, or differently textured, or more packed with those laboratory-produced vitamins that as likely as not have replaced the real thing which has already been fed to pigs, is alarming. They pervert what the science of nutrition should be all about; but at least the foods they meddle with retain some small element that is natural to man.

Not so with flesh foods. Here man is attempting to cheat his body outright. He is playing a dangerous game; almost as dangerous as the lettuce-

29

addicted tiger. But the tiger is committing straight suicide; man's game is nearer to Russian roulette. If he eats nothing but meat (especially Western man's processed and cooked, factory-farmed butcher's meat) he will join the tiger long before his natural life-span is completed. But what in fact he does is to adopt an omnivorous diet in which animal flesh and products figure to a greater or lesser degree.

It would be difficult to predict just how far any one of us can go in eating what comes unnaturally. The blood-drinking Masai will tuck into raw flesh and might be taken by some as proof that man can survive as a meat-eater. And survive, no doubt, he does. But while the Masai appear to suffer less from malaria and some other tropical disease than their vegetarian neighbours, they are far more prone to some degenerative diseases than are the Kikuyu, though among both tribes arteriosclerosis is for some reason virtually unknown. It is thought that the Masai metabolise their choles-terol differently (see Mann, G. U., Spoerry, A., Gray, M., Jarashow, D.; *American Journal of Epidemiology*, 1972). They also seem to have a higher incidence of intestinal disease and pneumonia. If they ate their meat cooked and led sedentary lives in a climate less natural to their species, their health pattern would doubtless be far worse.

The Eskimos have offered an extreme example of man's attempt to live almost entirely on animal food. Plagued by degenerative disease from an early age, the majority showing symptoms of hardening of the arteries far too soon in life, with kidney stones and urinary infections common at all ages, the short-lived 'emergent' Eskimo has proved a poor advertisement for his diet, while the effects of social change from increased contact with white civilisation since the Second World War have been disastrous;[1] A. Hoygaard (*Studies on the Nutrition and Pathology of Eskimos*, Oslo 1941) reported atheromatous degeneration early in the men's lives and that they lost most of their energy and fitness for hunting before thirty-five. Had the Eskimo not eaten much of his flesh raw, so ensuring a higher intake of the essential vitamin C, he might by now be totally extinct. At best one can only say that compared with the vegetarian Hunzakut, perhaps the finest physical specimen of a human being one could hope to find, long-lived and outstandingly free of disease, the remaining old-style Eskimo is no en-couragement to those who defend the virtues of flesh foods.

But these are random examples. Although of value, the reasoning behind such instances is necessarily empirical. Some people have lived to be ninety on a diet high in animal fats and flesh. Some have died at forty on baked beans and cabbage, their cholesterol levels no higher than that of a hamster. Neither example proves anything very much except that we vary in our constitutions, resistances, heredity, life patterns and temperaments. And lots of things that have nothing to do with what we eat can kill us.

But what we do all have in common is our physiological structure. Like it or not, the scientific evidence is that nature did not 'intend' us to eat meat, whether raw, cooked or in any other way disguised, and from this it is a reasonable assumption that a diet excluding meat and its by-products is likely (providing it is balanced and sensible) to bring us better health than a feeding pattern more suited to a predator.

Man is 'by design' neither carnivorous nor omnivorous. He is frugivorous, eating those natural fruits, nuts, shoots and so forth that we think of as the normal diet of the great apes. He knows that if he feeds one of those apes, our nearest relatives, on the wrong food, the result will be a dead or diseased primate. For some reason, our species and ours alone has the arrogance to suppose that it is the sole exception to a fundamental law governing all living things.

The reluctance many of us show in accepting this failure of our reasoning processes is linked to one of the many popular misconceptions of our time, namely that vegetarianism is only a minority fad. We are at all times tempted to believe what we want to believe, and life would be duller if we did not, but it is an indulgence that has contributed more than most to human misery, besides the exploitation and suffering of other species.

But times are changing, if all too slowly. Few people nowadays write off all vegetarians as a bunch of be-sandalled cranks. Yet until quite recently there was no recognition, even among many vegetarians themselves, that a dietary pattern that excluded the exploitation of animals was perhaps the most important step we could make towards the recovery of that ecological balance we are beginning to see is vital to the sane and healthful continuation of the world about us.

Acceptance of this fact can be helped only by the further understanding that so far from the exclusion of meat from our diet being an odd departure from normality, the eating of flesh is, as has already been stressed, a minority habit found predominantly in the affluent West. If 'cranky' is a fitting epithet for those who abstain from the majority's norm, provincial-minded meat-eaters who assume that the world ends at Boston or Ramsgate should think twice about using the word.

It is true, of course, that while all the higher primates are predominantly plant-eaters, some species on rare occasions have consumed animal foods; but these have always been supplementary to the basic diet. Although insect-eating is common among the lower primates, its importance decreases through the higher strata of the primate chain, becoming increasingly rare in the larger monkeys and apes. To what degree the first primates were insectivores is uncertain; invertebrates may well have figured high on their menus. It cannot be seriously questioned, however, that over the past 80 million years fruit, nuts, tree berries, shoots, bulbs and roots have taken over increasingly and are now the dominant sources of sustenance, supplemented by leaves, bark, pith, seeds, fungi, honey and eggs. The fact that the lower primates in particular still consume a proportion of insects and such small creatures as worms and snails is no indication of a truly omnivorous, much less of a carnivorous diet. Many insects, particularly those that feed on leaves and other vegetable matter, are in their consistency closely akin to plant life. Those primitive human tribes who to this day go into the desert or a delicatessen for locusts or a snack of ants are aligning themselves more closely with their primate cousins than with the tiger or hyena.

Although those who would like to prove that the other primates are as nasty as ourselves will always seize upon evidence that apes have killed and eaten vertebrate prey, such incidents are exceedingly rare in the wild and under natural conditions. Where reports of the killing of lizards, snakes, tree-frogs, rats, small birds and young ungulates have been made, it is usually the old-world monkeys (that is, those primates further from man than the great apes) who have been responsible. As Desmond Morris has remarked, meat-eating in baboons and chimpanzees has been hotly argued about. Examples have been given of baboons eating the liver and melkpens of goats and sheep, and while these incidents loom large for the farmers, 'they nevertheless play only a very small, subsidiary rôle in the general feeding behaviour of baboons. In certain regions they are absent altogether. The same appears to be true of chimpanzees.'[2] (Desmond Morris, *Men and Apes*, Hutchinson, 1966).

Chimps studied in thickly forested areas killed nothing but insects and ate no meat. But in broken forest chimps have been seen to kill animals, though the extent to which the meat has been eaten is uncertain. As Morris has said, we must not start running away with the idea that chimpanzees are primitive hunters. They are vegetarians – or, more accurately, frugivores, whose over-inquisitive natures may have led them a short way down paths for which a study of anatomy and biology tells us their bodies have not been evolved. In the apes studied by Jane Goodall, meat-eating incidents were extremely rare, and those she studied were unusual and atypical of the species in general, living as they did in un-chimplike surroundings. Unlike man, they have known where to draw the line.

Much has been written on the habits and characteristics of the great apes, and this is not the place to give them more than passing attention. But while in the present state of our knowledge it is useless to argue to which anthropoid ape man bears the closest resemblance, or to try to insist upon which of the hominid remains discovered in different parts of the world is the highest in the chain linking the apes and modern man, in studying the physiological and anatomical similarities to man, and the patterns of behaviour that are found in each layer of the primate chain, it becomes very difficult indeed to rebut the feeling that man, as the latest expression of the *hominoidea*, was 'destined' (if that is not too loaded a word) to be a total frugivore. His departure from that logical phase in his evolution can only have come about through some natural cataclysm of immense proportions or due to some aberrancy prompted by his insatiable curiosity.

We know well enough how perverted mankind's tastes can be. No great ape, given free choice under natural conditions, can match man in his perverse greed for substances and habits that are provably self-destructive or unnatural. Even in captivity, which is not the condition in which any species should be studied or exploited with hope of arriving at balanced conclusions, the willingness of the *Pongidae* to make omnivorous explorations generally stops short of consuming animal products. Only the most inquisitive, and therefore the most mischievous and potentially dangerous primate of all, has gone so far as not merely to sample the flesh of his fellow creatures but to make an industry and a cult of his deviation. If one has any respect for what few facts it has so far been possible to establish, the most we can say is that *some* of man's ancestors certainly were driven by circumstances to adopt a diet that contained an unknown proportion of flesh-foods.

So what has given rise to this idea that *homo sapiens* has such an un-relievedly sanguinary background? Little more than that aforesaid realisation that because the onset of climatic or some other natural change caused a local shortage or even disappearance of the food natural to the higher primates, a proportion of the human line relied to a greater or lesser extent on the flesh of animals. The proof that this was so goes little beyond the discovery of animal bones in and around human or near-human habitations. From this slender evidence the massive assumption is made that every trace of vertebrate life found on or near to primitive encampments supports the notion of man being a natural omnivore. Bone remains can last for many millennia. Proof of a plant diet is usually short-lived and far less easily detected. This doubtless helps to explain why we have been so over-ready to think of early man as a flesh-eater. We forget that a frugivorous diet simply fails to leave behind such obvious traces. Nor is allowance made for all the other reasons why animal remains might have been found in such situations – the attraction of fire; the killing by apes of other species out of curiosity and mischief rather than for food, and of course for their skins for clothing and other comforts; even a degree of early domestication of other species for purposes other than, or in addition to, their consumption. This is not to suggest that some of our ancestors did not eat other animals. They almost certainly did, though absolute evidence of this cannot be said to have been established. But a properly scientific approach should take into account the various possibilities that might modify considerably the picture we have of our omnivorous forerunners. The school-boy image which so many of us (including, it would seem, some of our most distinguished investigators in this field) cling to even to this day – the image of the cave-man with a club in one hand and the thigh-bone of some luckless animal in the other – is dying extraordinarily hard.

Even an ethnologist who claims that some apes kill will concede that the bulk of primitive peoples who have adopted an omnivorous diet rely upon gathering more than upon hunting. The majority of writers and scientists who have investigated these matters are themselves omnivorous Westerners and they may be predisposed to seek in our ancestry predominant evidence for our flesh-eating origins. I believe it would be fair to suggest that few scientists, no less than laymen, have entirely succeeded in resisting the distorting influence of habit, prejudice and wishful thinking. Indeed, to be fair to all concerned they have not necessarily been confronted with any obligation to show such resistance. We are all to some extent brainwashed by the ethos of our society and our times. The most distinguished palaeontologist alive was once a high-chair problem who had to be made to eat up his 'nice meat'. Once resigned to the habit, and finding himself in long trousers and with the obligation to earn a living, he went on eating what was put before him just as the rest of us do. Whether or not early man was a scavenger or a hunter, or both; and to what extent, if at all, he was either; and for how long and in what areas, and so on and so forth – these are still questions that are batted around in a great void of ignorance, half-fact, prejudice, jealously defended preconceptions, and the free-for-all atmosphere of a game for which no rules or limits have yet been agreed.

One significant point that the man-was-a-hunter-and-carnivore-full-stop school has almost painstakingly overlooked is that if that were so it is surely strange that he and his kind are not now to be found in the majority. The bulk of mankind, despite the hard-selling of American and European meat industries, is vegetarian – or near enough.

In any attempt to assess the historical pattern, the reasonable and more easily supported view is that in general man has obeyed the dictates of his provably frugivorous anatomical characteristics, his departures from this norm being the exception rather than the rule.

Among the authorities who have questioned the concept of early man as a brutish predator are Drs Lewis and Towers who in their reply to Desmond Morris, *Naked Ape or Homo Sapiens?*, wrote:

This tradition [of belief in early man as having been an aggressive, hostile, belligerent cannibal] is a myth, but many of us believe in it as if it were a universally established truth. Hence the further myth of our social evolution from bestial, savage,

34

prehistoric ancestors who were in a continuous state of warfare. Contrary to this view the evidence indicates that prehistoric man was, on the whole, a more peaceful, co-operative, unwarlike, unaggressive creature than we are, and that we of the civilised world have in historical time become more aggressive in many ways.

This vision of man's early nature, and the suggestion I cannot over-stress that the bulk of mankind has survived by holding to a natural rather than a deviant diet, are supported by what happened to such aberrant species as Neanderthal man, who was apparently the sole occupant of Europe in the middle of the Pleistocene period and the most violent and flesh-addicted of the hominid branch lines. What *did* happen to him? He died out. Some palaeontologists have noted this fact with something very like pained surprise. For here, surely, was someone who *should* have survived. He was doing all the right things, all on the right pattern of modern Western man. He was violent, he liked his steaks rare and often, he was convinced that force was what made the world go round, and his brain was frequently larger than our own. He had everything going for him. But bimbo! – suddenly there was no Neanderthal man. That he failed to make the grade might suggest to those open-minded observers who have not got so near to the problem as to be infected by orthodox storylines that he was simply unable to adapt to a highly carnivorous diet.

Most of our species is to all intents and purposes vegetarian. If primitive man (successful primitive man, that is) was the flesh-eater so many people choose to believe on so very little evidence, we may ask how it is he has survived in the largest numbers as a consumer of foods nearer to those favoured by great apes than, allegedly, by such short-lived sports as Neanderthal man and *Australopithecus africanus* (the extinct, small-brained primate discovered in 1924 by Professor Dart who claimed that it was a hunting and carnivorous hominid). We might also ask how it is that the higher apes and most of the monkeys are virtually vegetarians, whereas we claim to be omnivorous, when it is undeniable that the physical characteristics of all animals can be closely related to the type of food they consume.

As the biologist and nutritionist Frank Wilson has written: 'If our combination of the tiger, rabbit and pig way of eating is right for us, then we should expect to be different chemically from the monkeys and apes. We should be more like that one exception of the Primates, the baboon, one of the lowest, nastiest and most stupid of that family, crawling on all fours, with a dog's face and a posterior that is the big joke of the animal world' (*Food for the Golden Age*, Daniel, 1954).

He made a good point. Most of the glib popular pictures of early man suggest that *Homo erectus* was synonymous with *Homo predatus*. The more upright we became, the suggestion goes, the more we slaughtered other species and ate them. Study of the living higher primates suggests the very opposite.

Lately, the son of the late Dr Leakey has been working on lines that seemed likely to fit at least some of the theories of Robert Ardrey – who subscribed to the view that that primitive double-act, the supposedly flesh-eating *A. africanus* and the vegetarian *A. robustus*, hammered it out in the savanna, *africanus* exterminating the less assertive *robustus* by the simple method, no doubt, of dealing with him in much the same way as he treated his next meal, though perhaps not to a cannibalistic conclusion – proving that the allegedly carnivorous *Homo* and *Australopithecus* co-existed, though for how long may never be known. Right up to the present, in a sense, perhaps. But more recently archaeologists on a Franco-American expedition have made discoveries in the central Afar region of eastern Ethiopia that put man at 4 million years old – almost 1,500,000 years older than those remains discovered on the shores of Lake Rudolf in Kenya. If confirmed as the oldest relics of true man, the notion of Africa as his 'cradle' will have taken a hard knock, though even more recent discoveries near the Olduvai Gorge in Tanzania have for the time being left the state of play at 'deuce'. And so it goes on . . .

As for the future, however many discoveries have yet to be made I believe that a more balanced conception of our origins is on the way and that so far from an omnivorous hominid being the forerunner of *Homo sapiens*, it will be seen that *sapiens*' true origin lies in a fructo-vegetarian being from whom later omnivorous man – from climatic and other pressures – branched off as an aberrant and (as time will show) temporary exception. That is to say, 'Darwin's' common ancestor of man and apes did not produce anything so absurdly improbable as a physiological frugivore that had a natural propensity for the diet of an omnivore. By all means let us accept that the common ancestor existed and that apes went one way while man (in his mental growth) went another. But we do not have to make the assumption from this that man was exclusively a meat-eater. It is more reasonable – more in accordance with the facts we know – to suppose that he did, indeed, branch off from the main stem, but only to make a further division (through *force majeure*, not innate inclination) when climatic or other conditions imposed exceptional pressures. True *Homo sapiens* remains a plant-eater while acknowledging that some of his kin have to get a bad habit out of their systems!

I am of the opinion that this is a far more scientific and probable explanation than the view that has been fed to us by the bulk of the Western investigators. Many known facts support it. For instance, while the development of a formal agriculture clearly brought with it the exploitation of both animals and the land, even the early millennia of what we think of as the civilised era of our history indicate a lesser worship of, or dependence on, flesh-eating than we find in the West today. Two small instances: The ordinary ancient Roman was a near-vegetarian whose staple food was wheat. Tacitus refers to soldiers who, 'forced for want of grain and vegetables to subsist altogether on animal food, began to sink under their fatigue', while on more than one occasion Caesar admired the fortitude of those legionaries who put up with a meat ration when corn was not available. Even butter was to the Romans a food for barbarians, suitable only (when rancid) as a hair dressing for Burgundians. Lesser pointers are innumerable. When Tollund man was strangled and thrown into the Danish peat bog on some winter's day 2000 years ago, his last meal had consisted of barley, linseed and sorrel. If such fragments prove little beyond the dangers in generalisation, they are of some value.

But so far as the argument of this book is concerned, the where and the how and the when of man's appearance is not very important. The facts that *are* known are enough to prove, or at least throw a favourable light upon, the points I am trying to make. It really matters not a hoot which of the evolutionary theories takes your fancy.

What does matter is that we should keep in the forefront of our minds that whatever climatic or other chance of nature provoked a proportion of our ancestors to take to the eating of animal flesh (a change-over that may well have eliminated all but the more adaptable), and whenever and wherever it happened, nothing in their physical structure was fitted for such a drastic dietary shift. What so severe an abuse to their bodily chemistry did to the health and longevity of primitive man, we cannot say, though it is quite possible that since meat was probably seldom more than a small proportion of what was eaten and was at least fresh and uncontaminated by modern breeding and processing methods, he adapted with more success than he would have done today. Because we simply do not know the answer to problems such as this, the best we can do is to draw reasonable conclusions from what we do know, and the one and all-important thing about which there is no doubt is our physical link with the higher primates, and what the higher primates eat. I have been deliberately repetitive about this because it is one of the linchpins of this book's theme.

In view of what is known of the toxic properties in decomposing flesh, with which man's chemistry is not designed to cope, it seems beyond question that its effect has helped immeasurably to brutalise his nature and turn him into the most cruel species the world has ever known. Other factors do of course contribute to mankind's appalling record, in particular to our herd behaviour during wars and other examples of mass hysteria. Brutal behaviour is not the prerogative of flesh-eaters. Hitler in his way was as

37

much a man of violence as was Winston Churchill – not that Hitler's vegetarianism was exactly typical either in duration or kind!

Commonsense and observation suggest that it is equally beyond question that much of mankind's behaviour is due, as Lewis and Towers indicated in the passage already quoted, to the growth of civilisation. That is, to the tensions and stresses imposed by excessive concentration of our own kind. The study of the behaviour of imprisoned and crowded rats has shown horrifyingly close parallels to human behaviour under urban and other stress conditions. That such factors, combined with man's addiction to bad dietary and other habits, account for most of our problems is at last beginning to dawn on even the most closed-minded.

It is difficult not to feel, looking at the world we have made for ourselves, that modern man may yet follow his Neanderthal ancestor into well-deserved oblivion. If ever there was a case for sticking with the fruit and nuts, man proves it. Whatever comfort and hope may be drawn from philosophy, poetry, music, literature and the other accomplishments by which we choose to distinguish man from the beasts, when we weigh the sum of those refinements against the magnitude of his pitiless and incessant exploitation of other species (and, indeed, his own), the contrast only emphasises what a very great distance we have yet to go before 'human' can be equated with 'humane'. We would be helped to do so if Western scientists, so many of them still obsessed by their vision of 'real' man as being an aggressive omnivore, could begin to work from the premise that *A. africanus* or *Homo habilis* (or whatever other name may be given to him) was, more than the gentler frugivore, the one to take the branch line to an evolutionary terminus. The way the world is going, it would make a lot more sense.

But man has proved to be unique in persisting in those very departures from his nature that eradicate his instincts – or at least suppress them. Just as, until quite recently, the tobacco smoker invariably got away with writing off the critics of, and sufferers from, his wholly unnatural habit as intolerant cranks, so the flesh-eating human, in a mainly omnivorous society, goes largely unchallenged when he defends his habit by appealing to the shut-mindedness and ignorance of the immediate majority who share his preferences.

But although few people in the Western world have not at least heard the moral justification for a meat-excluding diet, what is perhaps the main scientific argument for reviewing our eating habits is seldom allowed the permanence of print. Perhaps this is because while 'abstract' arguments about ethics and aesthetics leave room for doubt, any case that is made out on the basis of scientific fact cannot so easily be dodged.

We know beyond any supportable uncertainty that numerous practices are not good for us. Many medical and 'social' drugs, smoking, alcohol, urban living, pollution, agricultural chemicals, noise – these are but some of the aspects of modern life that cause stress and load our battered systems with impurities, poisons and a range of irritations and tensions whose long-term effects must be as uncertain as frequently the short-term consequences are beyond doubt.

But when it comes to what we eat, the conspiracy of silence has been almost complete, at least where flesh-eating is concerned. Much has been written concerning the adulteration of meat and the chemical 'improvers' and preservatives with which those with a rapidly decaying product to sell try to increase palatability and shelf (or freezer) life; the basic consideration as to whether we should consume flesh in any form is almost totally ignored.

That this neglect is in part due to our indifference to the undoubted sufferings of those millions of creatures that are slaughtered every day for our consumption, is obvious enough. However many of the deadly sins man has decided are irrelevant, it is indeed certain that greed continues, shielding our species from the temptation to examine any arguments that might alter its eating habits.

The fact remains, however, that in eating meat we are clinging to a luxury that not only lacks any justification, but proves above all just how profoundly unscientific modern man – for all his technological skills – really is. For who but a true crank could dismiss the following facts of comparative anatomy, ignored by those who want to continue to eat meat?

1 (a) After intestinal digestion, flesh foods provide an excellent medium for the development of putrefactive bacteria. Flesh-eating animals (the carnivora and omnivora) have a relatively short and smooth bowel permitting the rapid expulsion of toxic food materials.

(b) Vegetarian animals (the frugivora and herbivora), on the other hand, employ a quite different set of bacteria. Having relatively long bowels designed for food that gives up its nutrients slowly, what they eat breaks down by a process of fermentation, showing that what is bacteriologically suitable for carnivores is unsuitable for frugivores, irrespective of what degree of success the body may appear to have in making adjustments. It should also be noted that the excretions of vegetarian animals are less unpleasant and more often suitable for composting and for incorporation with soil in the natural organic cycle.

2 (a) Flesh-eaters have long teeth, and in most cases retractable claws adapted for killing and holding living prey.

(b) Vegetarian animals' teeth shape is different to that of the carnivores, as is the enamel. The teeth of the Primates are designed for biting and chewing and not for tearing flesh, nor even the lengthy chewing of coarse foods as in the grass-grazers and grain-feeders. Flesh-eating teeth are like daggers. Grass-chewing teeth are made for grinding. The teeth of apes, monkeys and men come in between. Man's teeth are perfectly fitted for the eating of nuts, fruits and shoots. The dagger-like canines of some monkeys and apes should not confuse the issue. They are for defence, not dinner. And although the rhinoceros and bull, for instance, can show extreme ferocity, their horns and other defensive equipment should not be confused with the aggressive armoury of the carnivora. The protection of mates, progeny and territory is not the same thing as the predatory attack of one animal on another when the pangs of hunger take control.

3 (a) Carnivores' jaws open and shut in an up and down direction and they gulp down their food in large pieces with little or no mastication.
(b) Most vegetarian animals have jaws allowing the slight lateral motion needed for pulping and salivating their food as a preliminary digestive process. Their saliva contains the ferment ptyalin (lacking in the flesh-eaters) for pre-digestion of starches in grains, etc.

4 (a) The mammalian carnivora do not sweat through the skin but control their body heat by rapid breathing and extrusion of the tongue. Excess moisture is secreted through the bladder.
(b) Like horses and human beings, vegetarian animals sweat through the skin.

5 (a) Flesh eaters lap water with their tongues.
(b) Vegetarian animals imbibe liquids by a suction process, not by lapping.

There are other differences. The systems of carnivora, for instance, secrete some ten times as much hydrochloric acid as men and other vegetarian animals, this being necessary to dissolve bones in the digestive tract. Another significant chemical fact is that carnivores' kidneys have the capacity to convert uric acid into allantoin, whereas man and the anthropoid apes do not have this facility. Proteins – whether derived from foods which are eaten or from the normal katabolic processes of cellular physiology – are broken down eventually to uric acid which is relatively insoluble. Excess of uric acid may be precipitated as uric acid or as urate stones. Carnivores produce so much uric acid that the kidneys have to take the process one stage further to the soluble allantoin. It is a reasonable assumption, therefore, that man is not designed chemically for the ingestion of vast quantities of protein.

Animal foods are particularly rich in these proteins. To monkeys and men uric acid is an actual poison. Its consequences include gout, arthritis, rheumatism and fibrositis. It is also highly significant that flesh-eaters consume their prey when it is raw and fresh, whereas most humans need to cook and disguise their meat before finding it palatable, some of them even preferring it in an advanced stage of decomposition. And if these further pointers were not sufficient evidence that the diet of the carnivora is not natural to man, the fact that the pattern of the organs in apes and man is identical is enough in itself to indicate that their diet should be similar.

The psychologists have produced ample evidence that besides being physiologically and anatomically more like man than the tailed monkeys the chimpanzee is manlike in its intelligence. The gorilla likewise exhibits strong manlike characteristics, though with differences that do no more than underline the differences that are found in the moods of man.[3]

There are still great blanks in the chain of evidence which links the origin of modern man to an extinct form of anthropoid ape, but such blanks do not affect the deductions we make from the anatomical and biological structure we know as *Homo sapiens*. Indeed, it would not be abusing the rules of inference to suggest that the whole matter of man's natural (or 'intended') diet can be put in the form of an elementary exercise in logic:

1st premise: Man's physical structure is closely akin to that of the great apes.

2nd premise: The diet of the great apes is frugivorous.

Conclusion: Man is a frugivore.

'Closely', some may reply triumphantly, 'only closely'. Very well, then, but we know of no creature past or present more similar to man. And even if the true missing link should one day be discovered, study of his physical structure will again only prove his frugivorous origins. The link between two frugivorous animals is itself bound to be frugivorous.

And because, physiologically, our nearest relations are the frugivorous anthropoids, anyone with a statistical bent and wishing to render a useful service to mankind could hardly do better than trace the incidence of disease among a cross-section of Western man and compare it with the conclusions of an equally impartial fact-gathering mission to a genuine jungle. For whatever justification we may have for congratulating ourselves on the improvements to physical health brought about by greater cleanliness and other hard-won commonsense, we are in some respects more unscientific than ever before in our attitude to the diseases that have been increased and even created by the burdens of modern life. One of the main burdens is undoubtedly our indiscriminate eating patterns.

41

Anyone who has had anything to do with animals in their natural state will know how fussy they are about what they eat. Many of them would rather die than accept food to which they are not accustomed. They have an unanswerable instinct to guide them and no critical intelligence to interfere. Man alone, bereft of the protection of his instincts, enjoys the doubtful privilege of being able to sustain life, with varying degrees of success, by the consumption of substances that the majority of animals would reject out of hand.

As the higher apes, and most of the monkeys, are to all intents and purposes strictly vegetarian, it is scientifically impossible and absurd to suggest that we are in some mysterious way a naturally omnivorous exception. To be so it is necessary for our bodies to be chemically different. They are not. While we have our bodies, we carry with us living proof that we are naturally vegetarians. More exactly, fructo-vegetarians. A great deal of our ill health is proof of the same thing, but we have only fairly recently begun to admit that this is so.

Even though the steak-lover may scorn fruit for being nothing but sweet bags of water, ripe fruits contain much sugar, and few can need reminding that a ripe banana, weight for weight, gives as much energy as a steak. Nuts, the pulses and dried fruits are also rich in calories. Before the days of cheap sugar and refined flour, the peasants of the Mediterranean would work through a long day of back-breaking toil on a handful of dried figs and a couple of slices of rough brown bread; the remote farmers of Greece can still be seen faring fine on a diet no more generous, while the Arab still lives for weeks and months on a quantity of dates and grains that would shock the surfeited Europeans. The continual battle for the waist-line among civilised people proves that our ideas of the quantities of food necessary for life are false – and dangerously so. Like the monkeys, we too can live on much less, and usually in better health, as the endurance of the Greek farmer and the bedouin shows. Much nearer to home, and in colder climates, wiser and more modest nutritional patterns are being increasingly accepted and are providing ample evidence that fitness and vitality are far more successfully maintained on less and better food. Indeed, if we eat, so far as we are able, what is natural to man, we automatically find ourselves eating far less in sheer bulk. The necessity to go to work on an egg (not to mention bacon, toast, cereals, milk, sugar, butter and marmalade) is a commercially-prompted illusion that even the French and other European nations know to be false. For the Athens taxi-driver, 'go to work on a nut' would make a lot more sense, as anyone who has crunched his way down the pistachio-shell-littered streets of that city would confirm.

It goes without saying that how *much* we eat of foods that are not natural to man is even more important than how much we eat of foods for which our bodies were designed. The poisonous substances which are formed in the intestines of people who eat animal foods are among the most deadly chemicals known, such as skatole, indole, tyramine and phenylethylamine. Although the liver does its best to render them harmless, such poisons are inevitably absorbed into the bloodstream, traces entering the brain and provoking headaches, irritability and other psychoneurotic symptoms. People living active lives in the open air are less affected than sedentary, civilised populations whose bodies become little short of cesspools of self-generated poisons. When Alexis Carrel said that 'food can get at the soul' he was well aware that the putrefaction brought about by eating animal foods bears much of the responsibility for the incidence of nervousness, neurosis and insanity, let alone the more tangible physical ills which fill our hospitals and television screens with evidence that whatever other benefits modern man may be deriving from our all too widely permissive society, he is most certainly not finding that glowing mental and physical health that could so easily be his birthright.

Yet although so many of us have become temporary omnivores, there is not a fragment of evidence that man's body has gone one step further from the primates' plan than the other anthropoids, and the time must come when mankind as a whole chooses between Eskimo and Hunzakut, as the first chapter of this book attempts to make clear. It was only because our primates' gut was shorter than that of the strict herbivores such as the rabbit and the horse that we were able to survive one of Nature's toughest revolutions, the advent of the Ice Ages. We have fared less badly than would many other non-carnivorous species had they taken to animal foods.

But we cannot push our luck indefinitely. If we want to increase our chances of really good health (as distinct from the mere absence of identifiable disease, which is about the best that most of us can hope for), we have got to stick with the rules. The rules are clear. No man is a grave. We are physically constituted to eat and derive the most benefit from food natural to the *hominoidea*. Every attempt to flout this inescapable fact adds to the probability, if not certainty, of our suffering from our folly and greed.

This is not, of course, to say that a vegetarian or any other diet can prevent or cure every human ill. As has been said, there are many other factors working against full health in civilised man. Yet the principal health determinant in our lives – the nature of what we eat – is largely ignored. Admittedly, even with our eyes wide open it is virtually impossible today to lead a wholly natural life. The strictest vegetarian, tilling his own acre and living in a loin-cloth on the side of a mountain in the sub-tropics, will find it difficult, if not impossible to avoid descending at times to the level of civilised man and his manufactured, devitalised foods.

All the more reason, therefore, for each one of us to go as far as he possibly can to formulate and insist upon an eating pattern that is as sane and truly civilised as the problems of living in a highly technological society permit. There is no single aspect of that pattern more important than the extent to which we cling to a dietary routine more befitting the pig, the tiger or the hyena than *Homo sapiens*.

Notes

1. The more 'civilised', urban Eskimo communities, largely created since the early 1950s, when industrialisation began to corrupt the peoples of Greenland, provide further sad evidence of man's loss of the instinct for self-preservation by obedience to natural laws. Riddled with alcoholism, gonorrohea, violent crime and mental illness, with half their children being born illegitimate and suicide of epidemic proportions, the flat-dwelling city Eskimos have moved a long way in the wrong direction since the dubious benefits of technology and the bureaucratic mind were introduced when Copenhagen became their seat of government.

2. It should be remembered in passing that the baboons, along with other such farouche characters as the Barbary apes, have done much to make men doubt their own frugivorous origins. But they are considerably lower down in the evolutionary chain than are the true great apes – the gorilla, the orang-utan and the chimpanzee. These three genera constitute the family *Pongidae* and are by far the closest of all animals to man. The gibbons, whose food consists of leaves and fruit, make up the quartet of anthropoid apes, but have been given the family name of *Hylobatidae* ('tree-walkers') rather than *Pongidae*. All four, plus man, comprise the superfamily *Hominoidea*, within which man alone forms the family *Hominidae*. If you make the rules . . .

3. If we are going to get down to the basics of these comparisons, not only are the teeth and internal anatomy of the anthropoid apes very similar to those of man, but the placenta and embryonic stages show the same agreement. The menstrual cycle in the chimp and the gorilla has the same phases as in woman, and in the chimps the interval is the same. Gestation in all three of the great apes is nine months and the placenta is essentially of the human type. The old-world monkeys have a secondary placenta which is absent in the anthropoids.

   The great apes' divergences from man, marked though some of them may be, are almost all differences in degree rather than in kind. In general the differences correlate with habit. While the apes have retained their primary arboreal habit, this being much exaggerated in the orang-utan, man has become terrestrial. The gorilla, however, has become partly terrestrial, so who knows where *he* may end up? The chimp is intermediate between orang-utan and gorilla

   The blood of the great apes has been shown to be essentially identical with that of man, while differing from that of the old-world monkeys, and it is of course well known that anthropoids are prone to many human diseases to which other animals are relatively immune. The great apes and men share a peculiar susceptibility to syphilis, and apes are almost as prone to typhoid fever as are men. In captivity, chimps are liable to appendicitis, that modern disease of mankind. The reactions of anthropoids to sedatives, stimulants and poisons are again similar to man's, which is further evidence of their indisputable chemical affinity. Even the brain is in all essentials a smaller version of the human brain, no part or organ of one being absent in the other. The differences lie in the proportions of certain parts.

Taking all lines of evidence into consideration, but in particular the anatomical, biological and embryological, the conclusion that physical man has evolved from a lower form, rather than that he made a sudden appearance as though by some special act of creation, seems inescapable. This surely need not dismay those who seek or suspect some spiritually evolutionary purpose or continuation for man. Origins are too readily confused with destinations in the game of what's-it-all-about. The physical evidence does not mean that those who contend that we are nothing more than brainy naked apes have stated the whole (or what may prove to be the eventual) truth. Only those who are far too big for their primate boots can be proud of mankind's performance to date in the evolutionary stakes. When one observes the rate (not necessarily the quality) of progress that has marked man's exceedingly short appearance on earth, and when one considers the millions of years that may lie ahead of us if we refrain from destroying ourselves and our environment before the natural cooling of the sun puts the adaptational talents of all animal species to their final test, is it not obvious that our limited, ignorant, perversely misdirected minds and hearts have so far yet to go that our present progress can be seen as mere millimetres along the road that stretches far into the unimaginable reaches of the universe? As our knowledge widens, the eclectic mind can perceive more, not less, reasons for supporting a spiritual hypothesis. The amplification of this assertion lies beyond the brief set for this book.

Four

To the Cradle from the Grave

When we are born we cry that we are come
To this great stage of fools.

King Lear

THAT TO JACK SPRAT
Tigers don't eat lettuce,
Men weren't meant for meat;
Monkeys, men or tigers –
We are what we eat.

THE bulk of the evidence suggests that man, so far from being the natural omnivore many choose to believe, took different dietetic paths according to the pressures of climatic, geographical or other circumstances beyond his understanding or control; it follows that our unthinking adherence (long after any era of necessity) to a flesh-eating way of life invites examination that is not merely based on practical and self-interested considerations, but also contains a strong ethical impetus. I do not mean by this our moral obligations to the species we slaughter for our food (this is discussed in another chapter), but rather to our own kind. In particular to the children we bring into the world and for whom most of us feel some responsibility to do the best we know.

No suggestion is being made that the majority of concerned parents who compel their children to eat meat have anything but the best intentions. They are merely repeating a pattern that is generally accepted by the society in which they find themselves. Few parents' memories go back as far as their own childhood resistance to the food put before them. Nor, let it be added at once, was meat the only cause of battle. Children are often reluctant to accept cooked vegetables, cow's milk, cheese, rich or strongly flavoured dishes, and many of the other foods that are the result of our misguided sophistication. Very few children indeed, however, readily take to meat, however well cooked, minced or otherwise disguised.

Well-meaning though parents may be, their inability to put two and two together at this stage of their responsibilities supplies most depressing evidence of habit overcoming instinct. It is a sad comment on our evolutionary progress that mankind can have reached a stage where even a mother, at the point in her relationship to her child where she might be expected to be

46

at the peak of her intuitive love and concern, can be so blinded by the mores of her particular society that the last thing she is capable of realising is that the food that has created such an aura of stress, persuasion and worry as surrounds so many a family mealtime might be meeting such resistance for no other reason than that her child's whole nature is demanding the food for which its body was designed.

Whatever screams and yells may accompany the domestic routine of our primitive relatives, they are not due to juvenile resistance to the weaning process. The gorilla, the chimpanzee and the orang-utan have too much inborn commonsense to expect their offspring to graduate from mother's milk to minced and boiled flesh, however craftily disguised by being mixed with cooked shoots and roots. For the higher primates under natural conditions, the weaning process is as straightforward and unquestioned as in any other species except man. The difficulties we face with our own children are entirely the result of our perverse sophistication, and above all our unthinking determination to force every new generation to accept society's traditional pattern of eating. To anyone with a responsible love for children or a concern with our blind repetition of habits that are leading our species further and further away from its evolutionary potentialities, the sight of the human young being compelled to adopt the dietary pattern of pigs and hyenas is one of the saddest spectacles of daily life.

But it goes without saying that in the grossly unnatural world we have made for ourselves, even the most enlightened mother can have problems. Many Western women find they are unable to breast-feed at all. Time, availability of alternatives, orthodox pressures from relatives and clinics, these and other factors can make life a lot more complicated than the instinctive routine of the jungle. But while the responsible modern mother deserves every sympathy for her efforts to do the right thing, these factors increase rather than reduce her obligation to do all she can to make the transition from breast, dried or liquid cow's milk to solid foods as painless and natural as possible.

While it would be generalising to say that all infants readily and in every circumstance accept the more natural changeover from breast milk to those nut creams mixed with pulped, sweet ripe fruits or honey; non-processed cereals; shredded raw root and leaf vegetables; dried fruits, etc., that give them all they need without the addition of any cow's milk, dairy products, meat, meat extracts or manufactured preparations, there is no doubt that the chances of 'transition tantrums' are greatly reduced by introducing children to the foods to which their chemistry was intended to respond. How odd, when one thinks about it for a moment, that we should ever have supposed otherwise! What can complicate matters is if they are already joined in battle with their mothers through being forced to accept the far less digestible cow's milk (intended by nature only for calves) and those tinned and packeted preparations that are at best a second-class substitute for the right natural food. To their lasting shame, some nutritionists have even shown such ignorance and irresponsibility as to suggest that the Battle of the Plate should be won by lacing each dish with white sugar, so further widening the gulf between the child and those natural fruits whence all needed sweetening can be derived. Once the pattern of persuasion, deceit and force is established, every subsequent stage can be fraught with difficulties. This is evidence only of the problems we have created for ourselves by centuries of bad habits; the absurdity of modern man is that most of us have to learn how to do what should come naturally – and not only in matters centred on the stomach, if the boom in how-to-do-it sex books is anything to go by.

But most of us have long thought we know better than nature and are determined that our young should conform. So every orthodox book on child rearing plugs the necessity to introduce meat into an infant's diet as early as possible. By their own lights such authorities are at least being logical here; unless a child can be coaxed, bullied and bribed into eating meat early in life, he will seldom take to it after a decent interval of consuming food nearer to what his chemistry demands. Most such books take it for granted that infants have to be coaxed and cajoled to accept solids, as though this was a perfectly natural phenomenon. How many mothers, especially with their first child, have gone nearly demented with worry over the difficulty of getting enough food down the infant throat to cover a penny? There can be few parents in the so-called civilised world who do not know this to be so. Orthodoxy has for long been at pains to hide from them the reason why. Not rocking the boat is for most of us more important than knowledge of how best to rock the cradle.

And the sad thing is that it is all so totally unnecessary. Let us go a little further back in the light of the fact that even orthodox medicine often advises expectant mothers to reduce their consumption of meat, recognising that flesh foods leave much to be desired in pregnancy.

For over thirty years the late Dr Cyril Pink, a foremost nutritionist, did work at the Stonefield Nursing Home that gave conclusive evidence that a vegetarian diet before childbirth is beneficial both to the child and its mother. Some 4000 mothers were observed during pregnancy and were kept in touch with subsequently for ten or more years. Pink concluded that 'the ideal diet for pregnancy is not much different from that which is ideal for man and woman at other times. The principles are the same, but it is even more worthwhile to put them into practice. It is best to eat mainly fruit, salads, nuts and vegetables, with some cereal; at least half of the day's food should be taken fresh and uncooked.' In the absence of fruit and nuts, he suggested that dairy products and eggs be taken in moderation. Since Pink's day innumerable nutritionists, paediatricians and other specialists have learned the wisdom of this advice, and mothers put on a vegetarian diet, even shortly before the birth of their babies, have gained in health and exuberance. There has also been a marked tendency for earlier deliveries, many of these being without the help of anaesthetics.

The milk that a mother gives to her child when at the breast is a very special liquid, containing a unique balance of vitamins, proteins and carbo-hydrates. It is mere common sense that the subsequent weaning period should introduce the child to a full adult diet via substances that chemically, and in texture and taste, bridge the gap between breast-milk and solids as gently and naturally as possible. It is nothing less than a form of vio-lence to attempt to win children over to the toxic poisons, the coarse flavour and the unsympathetic texture of animal flesh. As Geoffrey L. Rudd wrote in *Why Kill for Food?* '. . . it is only the persistence of the mother which overcomes this natural resistance to the first doses of meat and fish. The child becomes conditioned and finally accepts the nasty smells and tastes. In this way most of us become meat-eaters, not from choice but from early conditioning; it is only when our reasoning powers are de-veloped that we can assess the possible advantages of an alternative diet, and by this time most of us are creatures of habit and just carry on.'

Writers more qualified than I have written on the health aspects of a vegetarian diet in childhood, but irrespective of the medical and statistical evidence (which seems entirely to support the argument of this book) I am convinced from lifelong observation of my own children (second genera-tion vegetarians on their father's side) and those of both vegetarian and meat-eating friends, that not only are vegetarian children of healthy stock as physically fit, mentally alert and full of high spirits as any omnivorously reared contemporaries, but that in their complexions, in the incidence of childish complaints, in the gentleness of their natures, and in their all-round air of well-being and general stability, the children who have fol-lowed the more natural eating pattern – provided it has been balanced and nutritionally sound – are ahead of the rest.

This is of course a generalisation, and no generalisation is entirely satisfactory. Factors other than diet invariably have to be taken into ac-count. There are exceptions to every sweeping statement, and it will be noted that I have inserted the qualification 'of healthy stock'. Much unfair criticism of vegetarian practice has been prompted by the observation of people who with some chronic illness or inherent constitutional weakness have after years of flesh-eating turned to vegetarianism, all too often as a last resort. For such unfortunates, or their children, to be judged as typical vegetarians, or as evidence of the efficacy of a flesh-excluding diet, is of course absurd and unreasonable. Vegetarianism is not some miracle-working panacea, capable of reversing over-night the abuses or sicknesses of a lifetime. It is (or should be) part of a way of life from which most of us have departed with varying degrees of success or disaster. To regard it, as some do who occasionally submit to a fortnight's treatment on a health farm, as a kind of confessional for the body, guaranteed to cleanse the system prior to a further term of indulgence, is to get hold of the wrong end of a very frail stick.

Support for the argument that a natural diet is our right even before our birth could make this chapter far longer than it needs to be. Among other points that could be made is the fact that schools catering partly or entirely for vegetarian children have achieved impressive results in physical fitness, sporting records and academic results. But what says more than words or examples is that there is not a shred of evidence for a balanced vegetarian or vegan diet being *in*advisable for children of all ages; on the contrary, all the evidence supports the opposite – that the correct food from cradle to grave significantly increases the human being's chances of full health and vitality. While there is ample evidence that the consumption of meat carries danger for any frugivorous species, it is logical to assume that a natural diet must be innocent of any conceivable harm. *Argumentum ad judicium.*

However, meat is only one – though a large – part of an omnivorous human's diet, and it is obviously not possible to pin on to any one substance the entire responsibility for a particular sickness, deficiency, or reduction in vitality and well-being. It would be absurd to imagine that by eliminating just one item from our diet we can protect ourselves against all the consequences of our civilised eating patterns. The very best that most of us can do is to ensure that from childhood onwards we get as near as we can to the kind of food for which our bodies were designed.[1]

What deceives so many parents into accepting for their children substances about which a moment's rational thought would arouse the deepest doubt, is that all young animals are equipped by nature to withstand at least some of the vicissitudes of early life. Built into our very chemistry are safeguards against the hazards of the exploratory and growing period, so that substances which in adult years might well lay us low, can be to a lesser or greater degree absorbed without apparent harm when the tide of youth is running full and strong. Just as an apple tree that has its roots shortened by a careless ploughman, or its bark stripped by sheep, will put out more blossoms than its unmolested neighbour, so nature rallies to ensure that when a species is threatened by war, disease, injury or other untoward circumstance, the maximum chance of survival is provided. As the tree strives for a heavier crop of fruit that will produce more seeds for self-perpetuation, in the same way the human or animal is given every opportunity to reproduce its kind. But nature is less concerned about what happens to it subsequently. Reproduction is given priority over longevity.

It follows, then, that the answer to our problems of over-population may well be seen to lie in our own ill-considered habits of life. The day may not be far away when we realise that the best method of keeping down our numbers is to continue to live our artificial and uninstinctive 'civilised' lives. Demographers and eugenists have already begun to suspect as much. But this is not really of much comfort to any concerned parent wanting for its child the best possible start in a life that will be presented with quite enough uninvited hazards and tensions without the added burden of self-induced mental, nervous or physical ill-health.

The bulk of reasonably intelligent parents are increasingly capable of looking at the white-faced, stunted, over-weight and sickly children whose staple diet all too often consists of little but fish fingers, fried potatoes, bottled sauces, useless mineral drinks, packets of harmful sweets and other worthless fillers, and of drawing therefrom their own conclusions. The question they should feel obliged to ask themselves, however, is just how much better for their children is their own dietary pattern.

This is something that can only be decided individually, but if in the light of what is being said parents are prepared to re-examine the whole question of their own and their children's daily food requirements, my purpose in writing this book will have been achieved. There is nothing greater we can give to those we love than the maximum opportunity to enjoy, and contribute usefully to, that life for which they did not ask and for which as parents we must take so much responsibility.

Notes

1. Among scientific research into the growth rates of children was that published in Albert von Haller's *The Vitamin Hunters* (Chilton, 1962), showing that vegetarian children have equal growth rates to that of children who consume a mixed meat and vegetable diet.

Five

Pathology or Hygiene?

It is a vulgar error to regard meat in any form as necessary to life. All that is necessary to the human body can be supplied by the vegetable kingdom. It must be admitted as a fact beyond all question that some persons are stronger and more healthy who live on that (vegetarian) food. I know how much of the prevailing meat diet is not merely a wasteful extravagance but a source of serious evil to the consumer. I have been compelled by facts to accept the conclusion that more physical evil accrues to man from erroneous habits of diet than from even alcoholic drink.

Sir Henry Thompson, MD, FRCS, in *Food and Feeding*

It (flesh food) is material which of malice aforethought has sedulously been rendered toxic during the animal's lifetime. In the first place his endocrine defences are interfered with by castration; he is then immobilised and over-fed, with a view to causing him to develop fatty degeneration of all his organs; and it is when this ugly process is complete that he is regarded as fit for human consumption.

Dr Leonard Williams in *The Practitioner*

The functioning of the mind is affected by food. There are certain kinds of food that supply the correct material for the activating of the mental process. Generally speaking, the mind works best on a mild diet, without meat, and containing fresh vitamins and inorganic constituents rich in calcium phosphates. It requires an immense amount of nourishment, highly specialised and containing substances secreted by the endocrine organs of the body, which must, therefore, be in a generally healthy condition.

E. R. Rost, OBE, MRCS, LRCP, in
The Nature of Consciousness

No physiologist would dispute with those who maintain that men ought to have a vegetable diet.

Dr Spenser Thompson

A CERTAIN amount has already been said in this book about the health aspect of a flesh-centred diet. Although I do not wish to over-stress this side of the argument – for I believe the case against meat-eating to reach far beyond the health of our own species – it does nevertheless come into the

52

debate at several levels and must be given appropriate attention, even at the risk of repeating what has had to be said in other contexts elsewhere.

As Geoffrey L. Rudd has remarked, one of the remaining bastions against vegetarianism is the medical profession with its bias towards germs and chemicals. Orthodoxy shows a profound reluctance to recognise the basic cause of ill health, and even to this day ignores or vastly under-rates the importance of diet. With their noses kept firmly to the grindstone of pathology, doctors continue to be given a traditional training that perpetuates a fundamental misconception of disease and the process of healing. It is not pathology (the study of disease) but hygiene (the science of health) that will one day have to occupy our schools of medicine.[1] Apart from a passing acquaintance with a few elementary diets for specific complaints, their curriculum excludes any serious study of the relationship between health and scientific nutrition. Undeniably, they are aided and abetted by most of their patients who would actually prefer to have organs removed than submit to self-discipline or common sense. All too many doctors and laymen appear eager for a panacea that will allow a continued disregard for the law of cause and effect.

Preventive medicine is still in its infancy, and with the medical world dominated by the molochs of the pharmaceutical industry whose profit-conscious concern is to promote a mounting reliance on an ever-widening range of powerful drugs, backed by constant high-pressure salesmanship, only the inarticulate sick have a vested interest in so unprofitable a condition as good health. Money may not be the root of all evil, but it unquestionably has a great deal to do with the path we have taken in pursuit of better health. Yet although no one needs reminding today of the dangers of reliance upon medication that is founded on the empirical opportunism of the drug houses, we are all caught up in the spiral created by that folly and greed which have so often combined to make mankind its own worst enemy. The general practitioner, constantly got-at, is more to be pitied than censured for his part in the conspiracy, caught as he is between the blandishments of the drug industry on the one hand, and the demands on the other of a public moving steadily away from first principles in its search for miracle cures that will enable them to go on living in the same bad old way.

No one would deny, of course, that some drugs have achieved striking, if not necessarily long-lasting, results. We are all glad of relief from pain or tension at times, even if the penalty for that relief is a wide range of side effects and a reduction in our resistance to later disease. It is virtually impossible for any of us to avoid being caught up on the band-wagon of a health-service that is founded on false principles, a remarkable ignorance of, or indifference to, alternative methods, and the stark and unwholesome realities of commercial enterprise. Though each of us may try to be an island, landing and embarkation points cannot be abolished. But this should increase rather than discourage our desire to arrive at the same and wider answers by means that are more truly scientific and founded not upon the barbarities of vivisection and animal research, or on poisons that all too often merely repress symptoms and effect some seeming cures at the expense of lowered general health and resistance, but upon the sane and basic principles of good health. These are simple enough – that we should eat and live in the least artificial and stress-producing circumstances we possibly can. Nothing else can begin to bring us nearer to realising the kind of health we must all want for ourselves and our children.

We have seen that a body, like an engine, needs the fuel for which it was designed. Fruits and nuts are the natural diet of man, as the instinctive inclinations of our children should alone be enough to show us without the scientific evidence that is so amply available. But as this is the age of statistics and evidential data it may be of interest to study some instances of the clear superiority of a vegetarian diet over meat in regard to health and endurance. I am indebted for much of my material to Nathaniel Altman's excellent book *Eating for Life* – an up-to-date and succinct résumé of the basic facts of vegetarianism.

Among the studies that have taken place in developing regions of the world in an attempt to evaluate the diets and nutritional level of selected groups of people in rural areas, was one published in *The American Journal of Public Health* after a research team had visited Mexico. They reported that 'studies of the nutritional status of several population groups on the high plateau of central Mexico have demonstrated that the common dietary pattern is fundamentally sound. This pattern is based on a liberal consumption of tortillas, beans and chili peppers, supplemented to a greater or less extent with foods obtained locally. The caloric intake is low and little animal protein is consumed.'

Not everyone wishes to subsist on tortillas, beans and chili peppers, but as one small example of healthy and hardworked people being able to do so, all such instances (and this is but one of many) have a certain cumulative value. A more recent study, undertaken in a remote Andean village by a medical research group from Harvard University and the University of Quito in Ecuador, found that many of the 400 townspeople over the age of fifteen lived to extraordinarily old ages. 'The oldest resident was a 121-year-old man. There were several over 100 years old and thirty-eight over the age of seventy-five. Of these thirty-eight, electrocardiogram studies were done on the twenty oldest, and only two showed any evidence of heart disease.' The article, which appeared in the *New York Times* on 22 April 1971, went on to say that Dr Campbell Moses, medical director of the

American Heart Association, called the findings 'extraordinary' and said that such electrocardiogram studies of a similarly elderly population in the United States 'would show 95 per cent with cardiovascular disease'. It might be said that Dr Campbell Moses's amazement was much more extraordinary than the findings, which merely bear out facts that are well known and in line with what may be logically anticipated in the study of any group that is living as were these Andeans, on a basically pure vegetarian diet.

This example correlates with our knowledge of the Hunzakuts of Kashmir. Many accounts of these people have been given over the years, but one of the more impeccable pieces of orthodox information came from Major-General Sir Robert McCarrison, biochemist and physician to King George VI, who lived and worked with them in 1939. The Hunzakuts are known throughout the world for their longevity and freedom from disease. Their diet consists mainly of whole grains, fresh fruits, vegetables, goat milk and distinctly natural water. Their occasional indulgence in goat meat on feast days can hardly be taken into account. Dr McCarrison wrote: 'I never saw a case of asthenic dyspepsia, of gastric or duodenal ulcer, of appendicitis, or mucus colitis, or cancer ... Among these people the abdomen oversensitive to nerve-impressions, to fatigue, anxiety or cold was unknown.'

The Hunzakuts are perhaps nearer than most primitive people to Rousseau's over-idealised concept of the 'noble savage'. An erect, finely built people, as 'healthy as the wild fig tree', and tireless and fearless of old age and even death, they have done so well not merely on a diet that virtually excludes meat but on natural foods that although of plant origin are not by any means all that close to the preferred eating habits of the higher primates. Living as they do in the Himalayan passes, where fruits other than highly valued apricots are not plentiful, they have had to use their intelligence to conquer the poverty of nature in that part of the world. Sprouted cereals and legumes are important to them, for these are rich in the vitamins found in fruits, besides containing several times more of the B vitamins than do dry seeds. A turbid, yeasty beer is a further source of these vitamins. As might be expected, the Hunzakuts are very particular about the cereals they eat, tolerating none of the refined, white sloshy rice of the Indians. The coarse whole grains are used, the proteins of refined cereals being inadequate for growth and the repair of human tissue. As is now well known, it is the germ of cereals, which is removed during refining, that contains the superior protein, for it is the germ that creates the new life, the rest of the seed or grain being merely a reservoir of energy – sugar tightly packed in the form of starch grains to take up less room. Much more could be said on these lines, but I do not wish to poach too far on the ground so well covered by writers who research into the refining processes and those other undesirable ways of tampering with food that are part and parcel of our artificial way of civilised life.

Another and much less documented group are the Tasaday people of Southern Mindanao in the Philippines, totally unknown to the outside world until their cave settlement in a seemingly impenetrable forest region was reached by a party of sociologists and anthropologists only nine years ago. Thought to have been cut off from communication for anything from 600 to 2000 years, the Tasadays' way of life is that of the stone age, yet in no way supporting the glib popular concept of the club-swinging, steak-chewing, aggressive caveman. The Tasadays lack all belligerence. Their investigators found that small animals, birds, bats, insects and even venomous spiders shared their caves. It did not occur to the Tasadays to drive them out. As for the killing of animals for food, this was an unknown barbarism until the intrusion of a hunter from another tribe in 1966. It was this man, a southern Filipino, who forged the first link between the Tasadays and the outside world. He directed the expedition led by Manuel Elizalde, the Philippines' Presidential Adviser on National Minorities. The discovery of this small tribe of forgotten – more precisely, never before known – people is another piece of evidence, if more were needed, of the nonsense talked by those anthropological theorists who try to make out that 'natural man' is a vicious, meat-eating predator.

By Western standards the Tasadays' diet is of course 'deficient'. They forage inside a radius of under three miles in the rugged, heavily-forested mountains that follow the general southeast-northwest axis of the Cotaboto coastline, eating wild fruit and large, pinkish flowers which are usually consumed on the spot. Before the Filipino hunter arrived, their staple food was a kind of wild yam, but the Filipino introduced them to *natek*, made from the starch and liquid that can be extracted from the pith of the palm tree and eaten either hot or (in the form of small cakes) cold. Raw or cooked palm cabbage is a frequent food, as are roasted green wild bananas. Although they catch and roast tadpoles, frogs, crabs and small fish, they do not even bother to eat the eggs of the birds which nest in their caves. If sickness comes they know instinctively which herbs may help recovery.

But although they lack salt and would appear to be limited in their diet by comparison with those arboreal primates who have a free run of the sun-reaching higher shoots and fruits that are available to the nippier species, the Tasadays were found to be in superb physical condition. The research team found only a few goitres and a single case of ringworm. Strictly monogamous, at childbirth only the wife and husband are present, the husband severing the umbilical cord and burying the placenta.

Until introduced to steel-bladed *bolos*, they used axes and other tools made from stone for such jobs as crushing the shell of the wild ginger fruit, hacking at banana stems and trunks, mashing betel nuts, pounding bark, splitting firewood, and so forth. Pebbles are split and rubbed against each other to make a cutting edge. Wooden knives, scrapers, digging sticks and fire-drills are their other main implements. But none of these is used for the sanguinary activities with which such tools have invariably been associated in our study of stone-age man. The Tasadays were found to be a loving and gentle people, lacking weapons and apparently any aggressive instincts. Greed is as unknown to them as real hunger. In scarcity the children are given priority, but the team found no clear structure of responsibilities and no apparent leadership.

What will happen to the Tasadays is anyone's guess. Their future lies in the hands of Dr Godofredo Alcasid, director of the Philippine National Museum, and reputedly a wise and humane man. Possibly the worst long-term threat comes from the logging companies, for the forest provides the Tasadays with all their necessities – their vegetarian food, their herbal medicines, and the raw material from which they fashion their artefacts. The outlook is serious, not only for the Tasadays but for the whole range of cultural minorities that are known to be distributed throughout the archipelago, some of the groups being hardly more technically advanced than the Tasadays. It is greatly to be hoped that, without exploitation and interference with their life-style, information about such people will be more widely disseminated, for such living examples are a more powerful argument for the truth of man's natural diet than any number of fossilised bones.

Although their numbers are steadily eroded by the infiltration of Western habits, the peasants of many parts of the world follow a pattern that has much in common with the Hunzakuts and the Tasadays and has been little changed for centuries past. Coarse porridge, bread, thick vegetable soups, with in some cases meat featuring on ceremonial occasions – this has for long been the basic diet of many millions of the world's poorer populations. We do not have to follow so spartan a pattern, but if the inhabitants of parts of Bulgaria, Italy, Spain, southern Russia and elsewhere can experience robust health, boundless energy and often long life, on whole-grain cereals, fresh and sun-dried fruits and other plant foods, how little excuse have we to bridle at a similar routine when most of us can afford to add so many more tempting non-flesh items to such a diet?[2]

Research into flesh-excluding or flesh-reduced diets has also been undertaken in more economically advanced areas during times of national crisis. One such study took place in Denmark during the Allied Blockade of the First World War, when all imports were cut off. Realising the possibility of acute food shortages, the government enlisted the advice of Denmark's vegetarian society and appointed Dr Mikkel Hindhede to direct its rationing programme. In 1920 Dr Hindhede discussed his project in the *Journal of the American Medical Association*:

> Our principal foods were bran bread, barley porridge, potatoes, greens, milk and some butter . . . the people of the cities and towns got little or no pork. Beef was so costly that only the rich could afford to buy it in sufficient amount. It is evident, therefore, that most of the population was living on a milk and vegetable diet.

The results of this programme showed that the Danish people survived the war with improved health and lowered mortality rates. In the very first year of rationing, the mortality figures fell 17 per cent. In the year 1917–18, 6,300 fewer people died in Denmark than died in 1913, which was the previous year in which the mortality rate was lowest.

The *Journal of the American Dietetic Association* reported similar results from rationing in Norway during the Second World War:

> Norway had a similar experience during the war years of 1940–5 when it became necessary to make drastic cuts in the consumption of popular animal foods and increase the use of fish, cereals, potatoes and vegetables. Strom and Jensen (in *Mortality from Circulatory Diseases in Norway, 1940–5*) reported the favourable effect of this restriction on the mortality rate from circulatory diseases, as well as the prompt return to prewar levels when the nation returned to its prewar diet at the end of hostilities.

It is well within the memory of all middle-aged and elderly Europeans that food rationing during the Second World War resulted, except where blockade or other exceptionally severe circumstances caused extreme quantitative inadequacy, in a notable increase in general health. This was not, of course, due only to the non-availability of animal foods, but also to the reduction in other (and particularly the refined and processed) foods.

Interesting and significant results came from a further nutritional study undertaken by Mervyn G. Hardinge, MD, of the College of Medical Evangelists in California, and Frederick J. Stare, MD, of Harvard University, as reported in the *Journal of Clinical Nutrition* in 1954.

In their study of 200 vegetarians and non-vegetarians these scientists observed only slight differences in physical measurement, blood pressures, and protein, albumin and globulin levels. The investigation included adolescents, pregnant women, and adults between forty-five and seventy years of age. Each group was divided into (1) lacto-ovo-vegetarians (those who refrain from flesh foods but consume such animal products as milk and eggs), (2) pure vegetarians (vegans), and (3) non-vegetarians. Nutrient and caloric intakes were about the same for all groups.

Although laboratory and physical findings were similar in all groups, the pure vegetarians were found to weigh 20 pounds less than the others. The lacto-ovo-vegetarians and the non-vegetarians averaged 12 to 15 pounds above the ideal weight.

Weight gains and losses of pregnant women, and average birthweights of infants, were similar in vegetarians and non-vegetarians. No evidence indicated that a vegetarian diet is insufficient for expectant mothers, nor did such a diet affect the growth rates of vegetarian adolescents who participated in the study. The report also found that 'there appears to be a tendency for the pure vegetarians to have mean corpuscular volumes somewhat higher than the lacto-ovo-vegetarians and non-vegetarians'.

The link between animal products (meat, eggs, butter, etc.) and numerous slight and severe forms of illness is sufficiently well known for even the most orthodox of medical text books to acknowledge the dangers and advise both the layman and his physician accordingly. To cite one example, steak eaten rare is helping to spread the virus salmonella, which causes acute food poisoning in adults, while uncooked meat has proved fatal to many young children. For the most part, however, such findings are presented so obliquely, so feebly and with so little follow-up that the implications are seldom realised.

Among the more firmly attested links is that between animal foods and those conditions caused by the deposition of sodium urate crystals in the body tissues, of which gout is one unpleasant example. Sodium urate, a salt of uric acid which is the end-product of purine metabolism, lodges beneath the skin or within the joints. This process produces the swellings and the hard white lumps that are a feature of this painful disease. As with so many other ills, orthodox medicine has concentrated chiefly on developing drugs with which to combat the symptoms rather than with propagating those abstinences which would remove the symptoms by removing the cause. However, because man and the apes are not adequately equipped by nature for dealing with the uric acid that is formed by the nucloproteins in which animal foods are especially rich, the relationship has not been overlooked by the more responsible authorities. Even as staid a popular reference book as *Black's Medical Dictionary* states flatly: '. . . inadequate exercise, a luxurious manner of living, habitual over-indulgence in animal food and rich dishes, and especially in alcoholic beverages, are undoubtedly important precipitating factors in the production of the disease.'

Medical opinion is divided as to whether an excessive intake of foods high in purines is the primary and essential *cause* of gout, for there is evidence that in the majority of cases the disease is primary (that is to say, of hereditary origin), but there is no general disagreement that animal food is an important precipitating factor. The red meats from hogs and cattle are particularly rich in purines, though such medical texts as J. L. Hollander's

Arthritis and Allied Conditions (Lea & Febiger, 1966) instructs patients to avoid liver, sweetbread, brains, kidneys and all meat extractives, broth soups and gravies. That desk-shelf standby of almost every British general practitioner, Sir Stanley Davidson's *The Principles and Practice of Medicine*, advises that treatment should include diet 'of a vegetarian type', while Conybeare and Mann's medical 'bible' the *Textbook of Medicine*, although not excluding meat and fish in moderation, forbids absolutely Hollander's list of precipitating meat foods, and adds fish roes and sardines for good measure, winding up with the advice that the diet should consist mainly of vegetables, bread, fresh fruit and cheese. One has only to read between the lines of such establishment texts as these, making due allowance for the fact that they take as their basis a pathological approach to health, a general under-valuation of diet in the treatment of disease, and a growing dependence on drug-therapy, to judge that if such authorities can go as far as they do in casting doubt or blame on animal foods, one may be pretty certain that their sorties in the direction of non-orthodox conclusions are marked more by under-statement than by its opposite.

When one turns to the evidence for a link between circulatory and heart disease, and a diet based on animal foods, the case is even stronger and in less dispute. In 1961 an issue of the *Journal of the American Medical Association* stated that: '. . . a vegetarian diet can prevent 90 per cent of our thrombo-embolic disease and 97 per cent of our coronary occlusions.' As is widely known, high levels of cholesterol in the blood have been linked with increased chances of developing heart disease, and no one seriously disputes that animal fats contribute powerfully to the presence of cholesterol in the human system. Referring again to the study made by Drs Hardinge and Stare, they confirmed that plant protein produces lower levels of cholesterol in the body than does animal protein, and commented: 'The pure vegetarians had significantly lower serum cholesterol than either their lacto-ovo-vegetarian or non-vegetarian counterparts.'

A further study linking atherosclerosis[3] with meat eating was reported by William S. Collens, MD, a medical consultant at the Maimonides Medical Center in New York, and retired Clinical Professor of Medicine at the Downstate Medical Center in Brooklyn. In an article appearing in the December 1969 issue of *Medical Counterpoint* Dr Collens wrote:

> American men killed in the Korean war showed, even at the age of twenty-two, striking signs of arteriosclerotic disease in their hearts as compared with Korean soldiers who were free of this damage to their blood vessels. The Americans were well fed with plenty of milk, butter, eggs and meat. The Koreans were basically vegetarians.

Among other scientific researchers to have explored the effect of a vegetarian diet on blood circulation in humans is Dr Oxford Muller, inventor of the capillary microscope. He explained that 'The influence of a vegetable diet presents itself in this way: The capillaries stretch out and their convolutions become straightened out. We thus can see that this form of nourishment causes a certain unburdening of the peripheral section of the blood vessels while the purely meat diet seems to represent a heavy burden.' (*The Vitamin Hunters* by von Haller, Chilton, 1962.)

Almost exclusive to human beings, atherosclerosis and such associative conditions as angina pectoris are marked by the presence of plaques of fatty-protein material which contain the cholesterol. Unlike many other animals, humans are able to manufacture cholesterol without the substance being present in their diet, and this is one reason why it is widely held that foods containing large amounts of cholesterol (notably animal fats, including dairy products, and eggs) may be a major factor in the development of atherosclerosis. The arterial walls, it is held, accumulate fats derived from the circulating blood that has itself drawn on the cholesterol-rich foods that have been consumed by the affected subject. This has been experimentally supported by the research done on rabbits which, when fed on large amounts of fats, develop these plaques. In world-wide surveys on humans it has been established almost without exception that people with the lowest animal-fat consumption have the lowest incidence of atherosclerosis. After the Second World War certain sections of the Japanese people whose former diet consisted largely of sea-food and rice and whose incidence of coronary artery disease was very low, began to eat Western foodstuffs. Some years later it was found that the incidence of coronary artery disease in these people had approached that of the Americans who had introduced them to their more sophisticated and unnatural way of eating.

It is well known that fat people are more prone than thin to atherosclerosis, and that there is an inverse relationship between undernutrition and the disease. It was found after the last World War that grossly undernourished subjects showed signs of only trivial atherosclerosis, and in many cases the condition was altogether absent.

Not only has it been conclusively shown that a reduction in the cholesterol level results from a diet that is deliberately kept low in animal fats, but it has also been shown that if someone with a high blood level of cholesterol accepts a diet rich in unsaturated fats (e.g., the vegetable oils), a distinct lowering of the blood cholesterol is likely. Business executives in the United States, alarmed by their first heart attack, have taken to drinking massive quantities of sunflower seed oil daily in the hope of arresting their atherosclerosis. Quite apart from the unpleasantness of such a drastic 'remedy' (for hefty flavouring is necessary to make such large neat quantities palatable), so unbalanced an attempt to restore the equilibrium is neither scientific nor, possibly, wise. Their more sensible course would be to adopt a diet more natural to their species, but doubtless many would prefer an early grave to going against engrained habits to so horrifying an extent. The main hope, as always, is more likely to lie with estrogens, anticoagulants and dilatory drugs, although the dangers in all such unsatisfactory measures are well known to the medical profession and would not be considered for a moment in a society that had not reached lunatic heights in its perverse refusal to face the absurdly simple answer to so many of its health problems, namely that prevention is infinitely preferable to any hoped-for cure.

With almost half the deaths in the United States being due to arterial disease, marked by a steady and alarming increase of ischaemic heart disease in all classes, but especially in the working class, in men under forty-five, and in women over the age of fifty-five years (see Davidson: *The Principles and Practice of Medicine*), the arteriosclerotic diseases comprise one of the major killers of our species. It has been established that not only animal fats, but also protein intake, have to be considered in relation to the pathogenesis of atheroma. The whole picture gets somewhat technical if one explores it in depth, but the facts are available in most of the established medical works as well as in the more popular presentations, so none of us need be in ignorance of the risks we take in persisting with foods that any hyena, but clearly not man, can take in its stride.

Unfortunately, such is our species' detestation of change, the vast (but perhaps decreasing) majority need such overwhelming proof that their lifestyle is inadvisable, that most of them are dead or chronically sick before they can accept what is obvious to anyone prepared to study available findings objectively. 'But it has not been absolutely proved!' is the kind of cry that is heard so often from the ranks of the habit-stricken. No one in his right mind could today suggest that it has not been 'proved' that smoking can actually cause (yes, bring about) lung cancer. Yet up go the consumption figures, hotly pursued by the cancer statistics, and still there are plenty of people to be heard protesting that 'Only a *relationship* has been established.' It is all a little like saying that when an unarmed man is pushed into the cage of a starving, tormented, but still robust tiger, there is no proof that the latter will eat the former, because their juxtaposition is evidence of nothing more than a 'relationship'. This kind of reasoning, if it can be so called, brings to mind the words attributed to the Duke of Wellington – an imposing and awe-inspiring figure of a man, the story runs – who was approached in London's St James's Street by a timid citizen who asked respectfully: 'Mr Smith?' Field Marshal the Duke of Wellington, KG, Duke of Ciudad Rodrigo, Magnate of Portugal, Spanish Grandee of the First Class, directed at the inquirer the kind of glance that must have levelled many an over-bold Chartist, and thundered: 'Sir, if you can believe that you can believe anything!'

As a final word on the heart and circulatory diseases, it is not being denied that stress of all kinds is understandably seen to be contributory. There is no doubt whatsoever that arterial disease is particularly prevalent in countries with a high standard of material living. To what extent the strains of modern (and particularly urban) life and the abuses of smoking, alcohol and the processing of foods are responsible, can of course be argued until the cows come home. But as atherosclerosis appears to be responsible for more disability and death than any other disease, and is the cause of death in almost all heart attacks and about half the deaths from strokes and sugar diabetes, the very considerable contribution made by animal fats to the pathogenic picture can only be ignored by those determined to live in cloud-cuckoo land.

The other great killer of Western man is cancer. Innumerable authorities have been at pains to point out that the increasing medication of animal feeding stuffs that is the result of our economic rat-race and the heartless profit-chasing that has produced 'factory-farming', means we are likely to be swallowing penicillin in our milk, arsenic in our bacon and pig's liver, and the cancer-causing female hormone-analogue diethylstilbestrol in those flannel-like slabs of tasteless chicken that have so inexplicably become one of the symbols of the Western *dolce vita*. In roast beef, too: as reported in late 1971 by the United States Department of Agriculture, ten cattle and sheep selected at random had been found to contain diethylstilbestrol residues 'in excess of amounts found to have produced cancer in laboratory animals'. Although now banned completely by the USA, Argentina and Australia, and banned for cattle feed in Sweden, France, Switzerland, Holland and seventeen other countries, Britain is still using it with the blessing of the Voluntary Veterinarian Products Safety Protection Scheme.

But regardless of the known cancer-producing substances that are injected in animals in the pursuit of greater profits and in the hope of combatting the ever more threatening diseases that factory farming and other unnatural methods of stock care bring about, suspicion has been directed at meat itself as a contributory or even causative source of cancer. Pathogenic bacteria are splashed from urine and faeces in the slaughter-house on to the flesh. They may also be transmitted by the dirty habits of slaughterers and others. Meat causes four out of five cases of food-poisoning in the UK. Cooking – all through the meat – can kill most of the bacteria, but raw meat can spread disease in kitchens, on working surfaces, etc. Shellfish may transmit poisons not destroyed by cooking.

Decomposition begins as soon as an animal is slaughtered. Its bloodstream, just like our own, serves as a debris conveyor for toxic wastes.

After death these wastes are added to by the natural process of disintegration, involving bacterial organisms which can proliferate every fifteen minutes at body temperature, causing over 90 per cent of all recorded cases of food poisoning. Cooking is not enough to remove the toxicity, and the germs which develop on pre-cooked meat and fish can be even more deadly. To give our system the additional job of eliminating another creature's unwanted material together with the toxins of fear that are released into its bloodstream prior to slaughter, seems to suggest, at the least, a very unaesthetic regard for the joys of nutrition. As is widely known, domesticated animals suffer from innumerable diseases – not only from cancer but also from tuberculosis, contagious abortion, swine fever, foot and mouth, mastitis and a host of others – and it would be naïve indeed to suppose that all diseased meat is detected and fed to our pets instead of to us.

To what extent human cancers can be attributed to these repellant facts of animal exploitation has yet to be confirmed, but the statistics are reason enough for concern. In 1970, in the United Kingdom alone, there were 117,085 cancer deaths, against a mere 26,721 in 1900. An alarming increase, making all allowance for population increase and any advances in detection. After bronchial carcinoma, cancer of the large bowel is the most common cause of death from cancer, and the one most often associated with flesh-eating.

As with arterial diseases, cancer is predominantly a disease of the affluent nations, and it is the second commonest cause of death among children. Despite the tens of millions of animals that are sacrificed in the research laboratories every year, cancer is also one of the most rapidly increasing diseases. If instead of groping for cures in the tormented entrails of friendly dogs, as Shaw so graphically put it, scientists had directed their minds towards disseminating a preventive programme based on saner and less self-indulgent living, untold misery might have been spared all species involved in the whole hideous canvas of suffering that is the penalty of our civilised folly.

As has been stressed by Dr Francis Roe, Research Co-ordinator to the Tobacco Research Council, one-time senior lecturer in Cancer Research at the London Hospital Medical School, and later Reader in Experimental Pathology in the Chester Beatty Institute of Cancer Research, so far from the causes of cancer not being known, as some have claimed, all too many causes have been traced of all too many varieties of the disease. Certain drugs, food additives, food contaminants, X-irradiation and environmental pollutants (tobacco, industrial wastes, etc.) are among the unquestioned causes. Such admissions from the bastions of orthodox medicine might get us all somewhere if they were backed by signs of a more fundamental concern for preventive measures and true hygiene. Instead, hope continues to be placed in such empirical measures as ever more sophisticated drugs and in the field of molecular biology. The concern is too much with how we can continue to do all the things that produce our diseases, yet somehow manage to cheat nature's responses.

Even those most concerned with not rocking the boat by implicating the follies of our modern way of life are agreed that cancer is not a single disease with a single cause, but a reaction of the tissues to a variety of exciting agents. 'Foreign bodies' – that is to say, substances which the human organism is not equipped by nature to accept and absorb – are unquestionably a major cause of malignant growths. While we may lack the kind of evidence that will satisfy scientific criteria that meat (a distinctly 'foreign body' in more than one sense) can actually create a cancerous condition in the human 'grave' in which it becomes buried, the knowledge at our disposal makes it quite absurd to doubt the strong possibility. By the exaggerated standards of proof some diehards demand, tobacco smoking must also be dismissed as a cause of cancer. Yet, at long last, it has officially and widely been pronounced that smoking does quite evidently cause the disease, though for years this was a suggestion dismissed as cranky overstatement by those who never wish to face the promptings of common-sense that so often become the hallowed scientific fact of tomorrow. An immense number of lives must have been lost, not only due to smoking, while we have hung around waiting for the experts to confirm what many reasonably clear-minded laymen had long ago seen to be the result of putting two and two together.

Irrespective of the fact that various substances cause, or (if the cautious prefer) predispose to, cancer,[4] it makes more mere 'sense' to suspect the rôle of meat than it does to dismiss it – especially in view of the undoubted fact that in the Western world today it is virtually impossible to eat the flesh of any animal, bird or fish without ingesting unnatural substances that the creature has itself taken into its system (sometimes with considerable cumulative results) through the food chain that links all species.

It is widely agreed that high-protein feeding speeds the rate of spread of cancers in experimental animals, and scientists have shown conclusively that cancer runs parallel to the incidence of over-eating as measured by calories. It would be foolish to doubt, rather than foolish to suppose, that animal foods, full of growth hormones and growth stimulants, contribute to the madness of the cancer cell. As the 'rich man's disease', cancer (long before the invention of chemical additives) was known as the Royal Rot, as it occurred in so many monarchs and those who could afford to eat the most expensive (animal) foods. The privileged classes have always been particularly prone to cancer and other degenerative disease, and as soon as such foods became available to the mass of the people, these diseases no longer knew any class barriers and descended upon rich and relatively rich alike. At least in days gone by our ancestors ate animals and birds that had eaten uncontaminated food grown on wholesome land. Resultant ill health may well have had more to do with excessive consumption than with parallels to the chemical hazards that are now in virtually every mouthful of flesh our species consumes. Nothing is likely to equal the sheer quantitative suffering we inflict on other creatures, but it is perhaps not fanciful to say that in our cancers and many other ills we may be experiencing that 'fruit' of *karma* that we have done so much to deserve by our unceasing indifference to the rights of the animal kingdom.

Pain and the subnormal functioning of the human body are nature's first warning that something is wrong, and as the vast majority of our physical problems are attributable to faulty living – and particularly to an unbalanced diet far removed from the simple raw, fresh fruits, nuts and other plant life on which we evolved for millions of years – it is inexcusable idiocy that the bulk of medical research is still devoted to the discovery of new drugs to obliterate and suppress symptoms, driving deleterious matter back into the bloodstream, instead of advocating the cleansing of the body's arteries by pouring pure substances into them in place of the effluents of our modern living. If you tip sewage and industrial waste into a river you create a sick and dying stretch of water. To create healthy conditions you do not dose a river with drugs. You stop pouring muck into it. Why should we treat our bodies differently? In point of fact we treat them even more badly than our rivers, for in refusing to avoid the primary cause of so much of our ill health, and in adding to the accumulated toxins the further poisons of the drugs with which we hope to nullify the consequences of our abuses, we all too often find that the subsequent reactions of our bodies are even more violent and need ever more powerful drugs to give a further illusion of improvement. A rheumatic fever patient, for instance, if treated with suppressive chemicals such as salicylates, may die later from heart failure or suffer with a weak heart for the rest of his life. But treated dietetically with fruit juices, such conditions have been cleared without after-effects.

As hardly needs saying, all organs from the brain to the kidneys may be seriously affected by drugs, for whatever reason administered. The final result may be long delayed because the body has great resistance, but there is bound to be a degree of damage because no organism is meant to have toxic materials introduced orally or intravenously. Their introduction places a burden on the organs of elimination, upsets the intestinal flora, the natural bacteria and the nervous system. It would take a lot of wishful thinking to dispel the connection between the fast-rising incidence of nervous disorders and the vast daily bombardment of our bodies by the wide range of pharmaceutical products that have become part and parcel of modern life. The link between specific drugs and vaccines, and diseases such as tuberculous meningitis, poliomyelitis, and a wide range of physical and nervous disorders, has too often been suggested to merit further attention here. My aim is merely to stress once again that it is surely infinitely more scientific and commonsensical to treat our bodies in such a way that the need to call upon drugs of any kind is done away with or at least reduced to an absolute minimum. It is madness and often suicide, as all good doctors agree, to court ill health by embracing without conscious reservations and abstentions a life-style that is virtually certain to have repercussions by upsetting our bodily chemistry.

Nor can this question of human health be divorced from the ethical aspect of our reliance upon drugs and vaccines. Quite apart from the appalling fact that the first children to be inoculated with a new vaccine are nothing less than human guinea pigs, anyone with an iota of compassion should be concerned that untold thousands of monkeys – highly sensitive creatures whose 'human' reactions and pleasures are often pathetically akin to many of our own – have to sacrifice their kidneys for the manufacturing processes, while yet more thousands have their living brains injected with the vaccine to test each batch for virulence. As Geoffrey Rudd has rightly remarked, 'anything so utterly barbarous, selfish and devilishly wrong in principle could not be right in practice' – a point of view that only those totally sold on the humanistic scientific argument can possibly rebut. Once science is divorced from moral considerations, we have opened the door to any depth and kind of brutality and evil – a realisation so persuasively and brilliantly argued by the microbiologist Dr Catherine Roberts in her book *The Scientific Conscience*.

The picture is not a happy one. Cancer, heart troubles, constipation, ulcers, varicose veins, migraines, obesity, diverticulitis, diabetes, and many other ills and imbalances, both physical and nervous, are increasing at an alarming rate. Millions of pounds are poured into research, yet hardly any of it into the investigation of diet. We take it quite for granted that this should be the case, though even medical journals have begun to suggest that somewhere along the line medicine may have taken a wrong turning. If the drugs and rivers of medicine which we pour into our long-suffering systems were one quarter as effective as their pushers try to make us believe, we would be living in surroundings that more closely resembled the Elysian Fields than a vast out-patients department. The crowding in hospitals and waiting rooms, and the vast sums of money spent on treating established disease, are not a testimony to progress and modern healing methods, but a thundering admission of our abysmal failure to understand the foundation of disease or to cope with its result.

Even if no more than a thin shaft of hope, it is encouraging that an editorial in the *British Medical Journal* of 29 January 1972, was able to state that:

> Nutrition is taught to medical students as fag-ends of physiology, biochemistry, clinical medicine and paediatrics ... The day is past in Britain when Edward Mellanby could change the physique of the nation with some spoonfuls of cod-liver oil. We now have to begin to learn the more subtle relationships that exist between nutrition and medicine, and how changes in food habits and changes in food production may affect health. Medical education must keep pace with the rapid advances in this subject.

Some doctors have been more outspoken and explicit than this. Robert Blomfield, MB, ChB, of St Stephen's Hospital, Chelsea, for instance, has written flatly (*Sunday Times*, 10.7.73): 'The fact is that the medical profession in this country has in general largely ignored the rôle of diet in the causation of disease, the emphasis being on the treatment of established disease when the damage has been done.' After condemning refined sugar and white bread – that 'bleached, softened, chemical-ridden, protein and vitamin depleted imitation of the real thing (whole wheat bread)' – he goes on:

> Most people buy what the advertisers tell them to as they, and the doctors who should be advising them, know no better. One has only to sample the average hospital meal to see how low on the list of priorities food comes in modern medicine. What is urgently needed is the widespread realisation that you are what you eat and drink and breathe, and that if these factors deviate far from nature trouble/illness will ensue to a greater or lesser extent. If a fraction of the money spent on research into the treatment of disease was used to investigate the relationship of diet to disease, the health of people in this country could be dramatically improved across the board. But much of this research is financed by drug companies who have a vested interest, not surprisingly, in drug treatment. And if one looks at it closely, so have most doctors. Naturally grown unprocessed foods ... are the basis of all good health – but, amazingly, this fundamental factor is almost, if not completely, neglected in British and American medical schools, where science rules the roost, as in our hospitals where investigations and therapeutic firework displays are the order of the day. There is an old Chinese saying 'Medicine is used when nutrition has failed.' No wonder the pharmaceutical industry, which spends roughly £300 a year for each doctor in this country on promoting its products, is doing so well!

Concerned about over-nutrition in children, Dr Barry Lewis, director of the lipid disorders clinic at Hammersmith Hospital, London, has emphasised that dietary prevention of heart disease should begin in childhood, research having shown that in the coronary-prone Westernised countries newborn boys have thicker walls to their coronary arteries than those born in relatively immune populations. The next stage, the depositing of fat in the artery walls, could begin during the first ten years of life. Dr Lewis also added his voice to those who have warned of the very high saturated (blood-cholesterol-raising) fat content of cow's milk produced by modern farming techniques. There have been several indications of late that milk is at last being seen for what it is – a grossly over-valued commodity within any society where there is an adequacy of other nutrients. The almost hysterical over-selling by the dairy industry in 1972/3 will doubtless continue for so long as this chemical-ridden fluid – in its pure state intended only for calves – is the by-product of an over-productive meat industry. But various factors can affect the situation[5] and because less affluent nations get little of this surplus, there is now a growing interest in the development of plant milks. Where a cow gives as milk only about one tenth of the protein she eats, mechanical processing can raise that fraction to 75 per cent, the milk being derived directly from lucerne grass, vegetables, palm and sugar cane leaves, soya beans, rice stalks, pea pods and other crop residues. As has been suggested earlier, such techniques should make enormous contributions to eliminating malnutrition in undeveloped countries, providing a nourishing liquid containing none of the dangers inherent in the normal 'pinta'.

Milk is not the only idol to take a knock recently. Even the belief long held by former 'cranks' that roughage is an essential part of a healthy diet is getting strong support from the medical profession. Many diseases are now suspected of being the result of too little rough fibre, including bowel cancer and even coronary thrombosis. Until recently conventional medical wisdom advocated a highly refined 'low residue' diet for diverticular diseases (suffered by 20 per cent of Western people over forty years old) on the grounds that roughage irritated the bowel. Now these sufferers, and that far greater number of people who have constipation, are being told by more enlightened doctors to take such natural foods as wheat bran. Even a raw cabbage stalk has been seen to have its place in the scheme of things.

Mr Denis Burkitt, a surgeon who spent many years in Africa before being employed by the Medical Research Council, has pointed out that rural Africans who eat bulky fibrous foods rarely suffer from constipation, bowel cancer and appendicitis, whereas city Africans and American Negroes who eat refined foods and often far more meat, suffer from them as do whites. Burkitt's view that chemicals manufactured by bacteria in stagnant stools remaining in the intestines for long periods may cause cancer, and that the presence of roughage encourages the development of a healthier bacterial flora, ties in with what a lot of 'fringe' investigators have suspected for some time. It is also significant that coronary heart disease and gallstones, both linked with a high blood cholesterol (gallstones are often formed from solidified cholesterol), are far less frequently found in people with a proper intake of roughage.

In 1972 one clinical investigation provided convincing evidence that unprocessed wheat bran will prevent much bowel trouble. Mr Neil Painter, senior surgeon at Manor House Hospital, reported that sixty-two out of seventy patients with diverticular disease experienced marked relief of symptoms and a regular bowel habit, without need to strain on passing a stool, after taking a bran diet. The majority of patients had had to take laxatives but were able to give them up.

If these examples are not enough to show that even orthodox medicine's attitude to the unscientific and emotional opposition to the diet natural to our species has become tinged with impatience, in 1973 the new family health encyclopaedia *Mind and Body* (Orbis Publishing Limited), under the heading 'Vegetarianism', presents an up-to-date admission that its profession is still lagging behind the facts. After suggesting that if it is more healthy to be a vegetarian this is probably because indirectly it may result in eating *less* (a startling about-face from the extraordinary statement quoted in Chapter 6 from *Black's Medical Dictionary* of an earlier decade), the article continues:

> Undeniably it is more 'natural' to be a vegetarian, in that for the majority of people during most of man's history, meat has been a rare item of the diet and vegetarianism an economic necessity ... Even medical authorities often insist that vegetarianism is unhealthy and veganism certain to result in dietary deficiencies. The evidence does not support these assertions. Careful studies have shown that the most likely deficiencies to occur – vitamin B12 and iron – are not found in even strict vegans. No doubt this can be attributed to the fact that all vegetarians are careful with their diet and take care to avoid dietary deficiencies. However, this does not detract from the point. Careless vegetarians, like careless meat eaters, can eat a poorly balanced diet, but a rational approach to nutrition avoids these problems. Another invalid objection that is often used by their opponents is that vegetarians are likely to become protein deficient. The assiduous use of nuts by many vegetarians is an attempt to avoid this deficiency. However, such attempts are not needed, because protein comprises a considerable proportion of the calories in normal vegetables. If a vegetarian eats enough food (even without nuts) he will get enough protein.

Although *Mind and Body* takes the view that the case for vegetarianism rests on moral and aesthetic grounds, their dismissal on scientific grounds of some of the sillier objections to a humane diet is a most encouraging indication of the way the wind is blowing. It may be deduced from other articles in the encyclopaedia that this light breeze of change has been influenced by the realisation that a humane diet is fast becoming an ecological priority.

But although such suggestions and findings as these would have been regarded as wildly heretical and way out a few years ago, we are still a long way from seeing general orthodox acceptance of the paramount necessity to study nutrition in the light of human physiology and the facts of comparative anatomy. The time is coming, beyond a doubt, if only for the reason that the economic and ecological problems the world has to face will in time make a virtue of necessity. And the sooner the better for us all.

But there must be a balance in all this. In vegetarianism we have but one aspect, though a most important one, of what may one day be recognised as an altogether better and more mature way of life. As things are, and in view of the many other abuses which none of us can avoid entirely, it must be accepted that vegetarianism cannot guarantee the cure or prevention of every bodily ill. But it is reasonable and wholly scientific to believe that in a natural and considered diet we have a better long-term chance of eliminating much ill health and creating a bodily chemistry that can better resist the many stresses and impurities it is impossible to avoid.

There is of course a place for modern medicine and surgery, even a place for certain drugs of plant origin (all animals know instinctively which herbs they need when feeling below par, and the human science of herbalism is far too often written off as a cranky specialism by those whose own remedies are far more suspect). It would be foolish to suggest that nothing of value has been learned from orthodox medicine, whose age-long concerns have reached beyond the sadly empirical, negative and commercially-controlled methods that unfortunately are the hall-mark of so much modern research. But we really no longer have any excuse for ignoring the implications of that wider knowledge of so many relevant and related matters that we have today. A humane (and therefore automatically more natural) diet is just one part of the new ecological understanding that has awakened in recent years. The diet natural to man is one of the most important priorities of our time, but it is only part of the new concept of our world and our place therein which I believe is beginning to be seen more clearly, especially by younger people sickened and alarmed by the environment they have inherited.

It is evident on all sides that thinking young people are increasingly opposed to the carnage and brutality on which Western society has been founded. It would be overstatement, or at least an oversimplification, to suggest that all the blood that bespatters the pages of our history books can be traced to the meat that has irritated and inflamed the human bloodstream. But there is little doubt that it has played a significant part. The decomposition of animal proteins in the unsuitably long gut of our species creates poisons that affect both mind and body. All other factors being equal, vegetarians are second to no meat-eater in strength, stamina, good health and longevity. But the suggestion has more than once been made that actual aggression – that misdirection of the energy that is natural to all healthy organisms – is more likely to be instigated by the latter than by the former. It would probably be profitless to pursue this idea, for examples

71

in support and denial would be legion, but on many counts the eating of animal foods can fairly be judged as the most pernicious Ice Age habit that human beings have yet to break. The savage, hunting energetically and helping his body to burn out the poisons, gets away with much more than sedentary, toxic, civilised man. As F. A. Wilson has said:

> For purely economic reasons many human beings gave up eating the flesh of animals when the Ice Ages ended, but recently the industrialisation of the food industry has enabled animal foods, previously the privilege of only the rich, to be eaten daily by the average man, and so modern man has literally eaten his way back to the Ice Ages through the carcases of beasts. As the cause of mental and physical sin, no wonder meat stands out with the redness of blood. Man pays for the sin of unnecessary slaughter by the slaughter of his own kin; the revenge for the horror of the slaughter-house is the battlefield.

To the battlefield he might well have added the hospital ward. Wild exaggeration? I believe not. Rather, I consider the time is not far off when man will look back with amazement at the day when in our ignorance, our selfishness and our cruelty we had the arrogant impertinence to suppose that we were clever enough to cheat ourselves and our environment, not only by eating like indiscriminate hyenas, but in seeing no argument other than the supremacy of violence, no virtue save the extension of greed, and no future except in the continuation of habits and thought patterns which Later Man will see so clearly to have been futile and destructive of the very balances and principles that 'civilisation' should have stood for.

Notes

1. Therapeutics (any system that attempts to cure disease without removing the cause) is not only the province of orthodox medicine. Most specialisms need to aim higher than the mere suppression of symptoms. The rules of natural hygiene make far more sense than most healing theories, though like all methods it cannot by itself solve every problem of the psycho-physical organism, any more than can acupuncture, osteopathy, herbalism, etc., valuable though each of these can be in the appropriate circumstances. The body's natural condition is health. Disease is the body's reaction to neglect or abuse. We have for too long lost sight of this fundamental truth.
2. At this point it should be firmly stressed that at no point is it being suggested that anything but an *adequate* vegetarian diet is being advocated. To quote nutritionist F. A. Wilson again: 'Only when man's typical plant foods are the mainstay of the diet – fruits first of all in abundance, then shoots, green and tender and full of vitamins and first-class protein, whole seeds by preference germinated, nuts and other vegetables, eaten raw as much as possible and grown on a really healthy soil – can a vegetarian [vegan would be a more correct term. JWT] diet outdo the mixed one. A vegetarian diet of over-boiled foods, insufficient fruits and tender greens, with

refined flour and other mush is very inferior to a 'mixed' [i.e., including dairy products] diet.' So let there be no misunderstanding on this point. It is no good for anyone merely to give up both meat and dairy products and expect to sail along in better or even equal health on an ill-considered alternative diet. Although there is no risk in adopting a wholesome diet that includes a modest quantity of cheese and milk and totally excludes meat, if both meat *and* dairy products are excluded it is essential that alternatives be provided. A chapter on veganism follows.

3. Arteriosclerosis means, literally, 'hardening of the arteries'. It covers three distinct conditions, *arteriosclerosis* (occuring in the smaller arteries in raised blood pressure), *medical sclerosis* (in certain arteries to muscles), and *atherosclerosis* (the most common by far and affecting the lining of the larger distributing arteries of the body).

4. Some spices, for instance, are injurious and are considered responsible for gastric ulcers and even cancer in Indians.

5. In the year 1972/3, in response to Government, total sales in the UK rose by 15 million gallons to top the 95-million-gallon rise in the previous twelve months. But by early 1974 the price of feeding stuffs had risen dramatically and milk production slumped badly.

Six

Values in Perspective

Flesh-foods are not the best nourishment for human beings and were not the food of our primitive ancestors. There is nothing necessary or desirable for human nutrition to be found in meats or flesh-foods which is not found in and derived from vegetable products.

Dr J. H. Kellogg

Comparative anatomy and physiology indicate fresh fruits and vegetables as the main food of man.

Dr S. M. Whitaker, MRCS, LRCP, in
Man's Natural Food: An Enquiry

That it is easily possible to sustain life on the products of the vegetable kingdom needs no demonstration for physiologists, even if the majority of the human race were not constantly engaged in demonstrating it, and my researches show not only that it is possible, but that it is infinitely preferable in every way.

Alexander Haig, MD, FRCP

It must be honestly admitted that, weight for weight, vegetable substances, when they are carefully selected, possess the most striking advantages over animal food in nutritive value . . . I should like to see the vegetarian and fruit-living plan brought into general use, and I believe it will be.

Sir Benjamin W. Richardson, MD, FRS

It seems clear from the work of the past ten to fifteen years that the mutually supplementary effect of the proteins from cereals, roots and leafy vegetables is such as to provide an excellent amino blend for tissue construction and maintenance. Of course, we should have realised this quite clearly from the records of vegetarian people which are quite convincing in this respect.

Sir Jack C. Drummond, late Prof. of Biochemistry,
London University, in The Harben Lecture, 1942

There are many alternative sources of first-class protein and the meatless diet can be as good as any other.

Dr Charles Hill, PC, MA, MD, DPH, LLD, Parl.
Sec. Min. of Food 1951–5, in the first Armstrong
Memorial Lecture, 1951

WHERE the last chapter was concerned mainly with specific diseases associated with meat and animal products, with clinical and field findings involving groups of people in health and sickness, and with the painfully
slow willingness of orthodox medicine to accept the vital importance of
correct nutrition, the more positive approach must deal in the main with
comparative food values and with tracing a brief outline of the vital inter-
relationships between certain nutrients – a subject as relevant to flesh-
eaters as to frugivores.

But the whole question of health and nutrition is so large, extending so
far beyond (yet often linked to) the place of animal food in our diet, that it
is possible to explore the matter only sketchily in a short book that is
attempting to present a more general argument for a non-flesh diet. Further
reading is widely available, and some of the leading authorities are mentioned.

However, those qualified often disagree most, and some of the statements made by people who detest or distrust the idea of adopting a more
humane diet are a good deal sillier than the silliest of its supporters. The
latter have, on the whole, to be more careful than the former if for no other
reason than that they are more vulnerable in a predominantly meat-eating
society. Many people must have been deterred from giving up meat by the
sometimes pathetically foolish advice given on diet in some of the popular
'authorities'. In one of the best-known of these, *Black's Medical Dictionary*
(1961), in the section on diet, one reads this ludicrous passage:

> The great objection to vegetarianism ... lies in the enormous bulk of vegetable
> food necessary, mainly in consequence of the relatively large amount of water it
> contains. Thus, if one were to subsist on nothing but lentil porridge, about 5 pounds
> of it would be necessary daily; or if one lived solely on green vegetables and succulent
> fruits, the impossible weight of about 30 pounds every day would be necessary to a
> fairly hard-working healthy man.

Such gems of nonsense leave one momentarily groping for words. One
has to discard the false premise and replace it by a factual proposition
before one can even begin to communicate. The lentil ploy makes just
as much sense as to point out that in order to get enough iron by subsisting
on 'nothing but milk', that 'fairly hard-working healthy man' would have
to drink 8000 fluid ounces every day. Just who would consider subsisting
on 5 pounds of lentil porridge (a dish, I may say, I have never even met face
to face) is not suggested, though it would certainly be someone far nuttier
than any vegetarian one is likely to encounter. Only a strangely ignorant
or prejudiced critic could suggest that flesh-abstainers would expect to
function adequately on so limited a range of primate food. He can certainly
never have asked himself what the water content of *meat* happens to be –
the percentage in lean, broiled steak is, as it happens, 59 per cent, and the

toxic wastes from the animal's bloodstream, plus the bacteria from putrefaction and often diseased tissue, make it very dirty water indeed – for all that the broiling should destroy the bacteria.

After which rather negative skirmishing, it must be stated – and unequivocally so – that neither vegetarians (lacto-) nor vegans eat, nor need to eat, appreciably larger quantities of plant or any other foods than meateaters. If anything, their total intake is probably less, for while many vegetarians may tackle larger or more balanced salads than most meateaters, and while vegans are likely to eat more nuts and pulses, both classes tend to eat less of the refined, processed and prepared foods to which those for whom greed ranks above need are apt to be addicted. Perhaps the best way to dismiss some of the standard absurdities is to study Table 3, showing the composition of various foods and based on the second edition (1970) of the *Manual of Nutrition*, published by HMSO for the Ministry of Agriculture, Fisheries and Food. The composition is given per 100 grams and reference to this Table will use the abbreviation (MN). A column has been added for the percentage of water in each food listed, and this percentage is taken from the comparable tables of the *Nutritive Value of Foods* (text reference (NVF) will be used), prepared by the Consumer and Food Economics Research Division of the Agricultural Research Service of Washington, DC, for the United States Department of Agriculture's 'Home and Garden Bulletin' no. 72 (revised 1970).

Comparison of these two tables shows some contradictions, mostly small. Various factors account for these. Allowance has to be made for experimental errors, for compositional variation between different areas of growth, for freshness, for the extent to which some foods have been dried, and the degree to which others have been cooked; it may or may not be relevant that that notoriously overcooked object the British brussels sprout rates only 16 kilocalories (calories for short – see page 83) to 100 grams in the (MN) Table, whereas (NVF) shows over double this figure at 36. There is a similar discrepancy for boiled cabbage, and both vegetables also fail to show anything like as satisfactory a protein content in Britain as in America. These differences – in calories, protein or both – may be seen in other vegetables listed, including peas, potatoes, tomatoes, onions, mushrooms and carrots.

Certain plant foods of importance are inadequately covered or not listed in (MN) at all, and the following values from (NVF) should be useful for considering alongside the (MN) Table 3.

Avocado. A 240-gram Californian winter avacado can afford 370 calories and 5 grams of protein. Also 37 grams of fat and useful amounts of calcium, vitamin A, the vitamin B complex, etc.

76

Table 3

No.	Food	Water %	Energy value Kcal	Energy value KJ	Protein g	Fat g	Carbohydrate (as monosaccharide) g
Milk							
1	Cow's milk, whole, fluid	87	65	272	3.3	3.8	4.8
2	Cream, single	80	189	792	2.8	18.0	4.2
3	Yoghurt, natural	88	57	239	3.6	2.6	5.2
Cheese							
4	Cheese, cheddar	37	412	1726	25.4	34.5	0
5	Cheese, cottage	79	115	482	15.2	4.0	4.5
Meat							
6	Bacon, average	8	476	1994	11.0	48.0	0
7	Beef, average	50	313	1311	14.8	28.2	0
8	Beef, stewed steak	59	242	1014	29.0	14.0	0
9	Chicken, roast	58	184	771	29.6	7.3	0
10	Lamb, roast	58	284	1190	25.0	20.4	0
11	Pork, average	50	408	1710	12.0	40.0	0
Fish							
12	Cod, haddock, white fish	66	69	289	16.0	0.5	0
13	Sardines, canned in oil	62	285	1194	20.4	22.6	0
Eggs							
14	Eggs, fresh	74	158	662	11.9	12.3	0
Fats							
15	Butter	16	745	3122	0.5	82.5	0
16	Lard, dripping	0	894	3746	0	99.3	0
17	Margarine	16	769	3222	0.2	85.3	0
18	Oils (vegetable), salad and cooking	0	899	3767	0	99.9	0
Vegetables							
19	Beans, canned in tomato sauce	71	92	385	6.0	0.4	17.3
20	Beans, broad	90	69	289	7.2	0.5	9.5
21	Beetroot, boiled	91	44	184	1.8	0	9.9
22	Brussels sprouts, boiled	88	16	67	2.4	0	1.7

No.	Food	Water %	Energy value Kcal	KJ	Protein g	Fat g	Carbohydrate (as monosaccharide) g
23	Cabbage, raw	92	28	117	1·5	0	5·8
24	Cabbage, boiled	94	8	34	0·8	0	1·3
25	Carrots, old, cooked	91	23	96	0·7	0	5·4
26	Cauliflower	93	24	101	3·4	0	2·8
27	Parsnips	82	49	205	1·7	0	11·3
28	Peas, fresh or quick frozen, boiled	82	49	205	5·0	0	7·7
29	Potatoes, boiled	80	79	331	1·4	0	19·7
30	Spinach	92	21	88	2·7	0	2·8
31	Sweet corn, canned	81	95	398	2·6	0·8	20·5
Fruit							
32	Apples	85	46	193	0·3	0	12·0
33	Apricots, dried	25	182	763	4·8	0	43·4
34	Bananas	76	76	318	1·1	0	19·2
35	Dates	22	248	1039	2·0	0	63·9
36	Figs, dried	23	213	892	3·6	0	52·9
37	Grapefruit	89	22	92	0·6	0	5·3
38	Oranges	86	35	147	0·8	0	8·5
39	Pears	83	41	172	0·3	0	10·6
40	Sultanas	18	249	1043	1·7	0	64·7
Nuts							
41	Almonds	5	580	2430	20·5	53·5	4·3
42	Coconut, dessicated	51(c)	608	2548	6·6	62·0	6·4
43	Peanuts, roasted	2	586	2455	28·1	49·0	8·6

	No.							
Cereals	44	Barley, pearl, dry	11	360	1508	7·7	1·7	83·6
	45	Bread, white, enriched	36	253	1060	8·3	1·7	54·6
	46	Bread, wholemeal	36	241	1010	9·6	3·1	46·7
	47	Oatmeal	3	400	1676	12·1	8·7	72·8
	48	Spaghetti	68	364	1525	9·9	1·0	84·0
Preserves	49	Honey	17	288	1207	0·4	0	76·4
	50	Sugar, white	Trace	394	1651	0	0	105·5

No.	Calcium	Iron	Vitamin A (retinol equivalents)	Thiamine (B1)	Riboflavin (B2)	Nicotinic Acid (B3)		Ascorbic Acid (C)
						Total	Equivalents	
	mg	mg	µg	mg	mg	mg	mg	mg
1	120	0·1	40(av.)	0·04	0·15	0·1	0·9	1(a)
2	100	0·1	155	0·03	0·13	0·1	0·8	1
3	140	0·1	39	0·05	0·19	0·1	0·9	0
4	810	0·6	420	0·04	0·50	0·1	5·2	0
5	80	0·4	27	0·03	0·27	0·1	3·2	0
6	10	1·0	0	0·40	0·15	1·5	4·0	0
7	10	4·0	0	0·07	0·20	5·0	7·8	0
8	8	5·0	0	0·05	0·22	5·0	10·4	0
9	15	2·6	0	0·04	0·14	4·9	10·0	0
10	4	4·3	0	0·10	0·25	4·5	9·8	0
11	10	1·0	0	1·00	0·20	5·0	7·7	0
12	25	1·0	0	0·06	0·10	3·0	6·0	0

79

No.	Calcium	Iron	Vitamin A (retinol equivalents)	Thiamine (B1)	Riboflavin (B2)	Nicotinic Acid (B3) Total	Nicotinic Acid (B3) Equivalents	Ascorbic Acid (C)
	mg	mg	µg	mg	mg	mg	mg	mg
13	409	4·0	30	0	0·20	5·0	8·6	0
14	56	2·5	300	0·10	0·35	0·1	3·0	0
15	15	0·2	995	0	0	0	0·1	0
16	0	0	0	0	0	0	0	0
17	4	0·3	900	0	0	0	0·1	0
18	0	0	0	0	0	0	0	0
19	62	2·1	50	0·06	0·04	0·5	1·5	3
20	30	1·1	22	0·28	0·05	4·0	5·0	30
21	30	0·7	0	0·02	0·04	0·1	0·4	5
22	27	0·6	67	0·06	0·10	0·4	0·9	35
23	65	1·0	50	0·06	0·05	0·2	0·5	60
24	58	0·5	50	0·03	0·03	0·2	0·3	20
25	48	0·6	2000	0·06	0·05	0·6	0·7	6
26	18	0·6	5	0·10	0·10	0·6	1·4	70
27	55	0·6	0	0·10	0·09	1·0	1·3	15
28	13	1·2	50	0·25	0·11	1·5	2·3	15
29	4	0·5	0	0·08	0·03	0·8	1·2	4-15(b)
30	70	3·2	1000	0·12	0·20	0·6	1·2	60
31	5	0·5	35	0·03	0·05	0·9	0·3	4
32	4	0·3	5	0·04	0·02	0·1	0·1	5
33	92	4·1	600	0	0·20	3·0	3·4	0

34	7	0·4	33	0·04	0·07	0·6	0·8	10
35	68	1·6	10	0·07	0·04	2·0	2·3	0
36	284	4·2	8	0·10	0·13	1·7	2·2	0
37	17	0·3	0	0·05	0·02	0·2	0·3	40
38	41	0·3	8	0·10	0·03	0·2	0·3	50
39	8	0·2	2	0·03	0·03	0·2	0·3	3
40	52	1·8	0	0·10	0·30	0·5	0·6	0
41	247	4·2	0	0·32	0·25	2·0	4·9	0
42	22	3·6	0	0·06	0·04	0·6	1·8	0
43	61	2·0	0	0·23	0·10	16·0	20·8	0
44	10	0·7	0	0·12	0·08	2·5	2·2	0
45	100	1·8	0	0·18	0·02	1·4	2·3	0
46	28	3·0	0	0·24	0·09	2·6	1·9	0
47	55	4·1	0	0·50	0·10	1·0	2·8	0
48	23	1·2	0	0·09	0·06	1·7	1·8	0
49	5	0·4	0	0	0·05	0·2	0·2	0
50	1	0	0	0	0	0	0	0

(a) less than 1 mg.
(b) Vit. C falls during storage
(c) grated, fresh

Dried peas, beans and nuts. These most valuable foods are hardly given attention by (MN), though dry lentils are admitted to contain 295 calories per 100 grams, with protein at 23·8 g and good amounts of calcium and iron. Split dried peas showing over 1 calorie per gram weight, and 20 g of protein per cup of 250 g, should surely have been included, as should lima ('butter'), haricot and other dried beans whose energy value and protein content are quantitatively and qualitatively excellent. It is equally regrettable that only three kinds of nuts are shown. The most important exclusions are: (1) Cashews. In their popular roasted form a cup of 140 g produces 785 calories, 24 g protein (unroasted 20 g), 64 g fat, 53 milligrams calcium, and other significant nutrients. (2) Pecans. Better known in the USA than in the UK, these excellent nuts (walnuts with zippers is as good a description as any other) hold 740 calories to 108 g, also 10 g protein, 77 g fat, 79 mg calcium, etc. (3) Walnuts. These come out at 790 calories per 126 g, 26 g protein, 75 g fat, 380 mg vitamin A.

Rice. Brown (unpolished) rice gives over 1 calorie per gram weight when cooked, and over 2·5 g protein per 100 g, but it has less value when taken in its white and enriched form. Much is 'lost' by absorption of water in cooking, there being 12 g protein to 185 g raw weight.

Soya beans. Dried soya beans, cooked, produce well over 1 calorie per gram, also 10 per cent protein, 5 g fat, and much higher amounts of calcium iron, etc., than does meat. A significant comparison may be made between a cup (100 g) of dried nonfat cow's milk, giving 360 calories, 35 g protein, and 1 g fat, and a cup (100 g) of low fat, dried soya bean powder showing 250 calories, 52 g protein, 5·6 g fat.[1] Soya bean flour should also be compared with enriched white flour, 120 g of the former producing 425 calories, 52 g protein, 8 g fat, 315 mg calcium, 10·9 mg iron, and 96 international units of vitamin A, against 115 g of the latter showing only 12 g protein, 1 g fat, 18 mg calcium, 3·3 mg iron and no vitamin A for the same amount of calories.

Wheat germ. Raw wheat germ has 363 calories per 100 g, 27 g protein, 11 g fat, 72 mg calcium, 9·4 mg iron and important mineral quantities. A very cheap source of protein.

Yeast. A tablespoon (8 g) of dry yeast yields roughly 25 calories, 3 g protein and high proportions of essential minerals and vitamins. Of great importance in food technology, not only for bread and alcoholic beverages, yeast – like wheat germ, bran and the cereals – is at last receiving serious attention from nutritionists and the medical world.

There are many other food sources that contribute to a balanced and healthy diet based on plant rather than animal life, some of them foreign to the conventional British nutritionist, yet important enough to be listed in the (NVF) tables. Dandelion greens, for instance. Cooked, 180 g of this remarkable vegetable ('weed' is an insult) give 60 calories, 4 g protein, 252 mg calcium and 21,060 international units of vitamin A, which puts dandelions into the top league with liver for vitamin A and above even carrots, spinach and dried apricots. It would also not be irrelevant to mention that brown (Barbados) sugar compares well with white, which is valueless except for calories. The brown at least holds 187 mg of calcium, 7·5 mg iron and small amounts of vitamins per cup of 220 g, supplying a more moderate 280 calories against white sugar's 770 (NVF); but we are doubtless better without either. This sort of reflection, however, threatens to lead into the more general area of health foods, already well covered in other books in the nutritional field.

Before we examine individually the main nutrients listed in Table 3, we might consider the question of calories. Calories are not nutrients, but units of heat used in expressing the energy content of foods. They come in two sizes, small and large. The smaller calorie is the amount of heat needed to raise the temperature of a gram of water by one degree centigrade. This doesn't add up to very much, so the large calorie (or kilocalorie) is usually referred to for nutritional purposes (see Appendix III).

As the (NVF) table shows (and comparison may be made with Table 3), a pound (453·6 grams) of broiled, lean sirloin beefsteak is needed to supply 920 calories. Take lean and fat and you have a figure of 1760. These are not sensational figures if it is calories you are after, when one sees that walnuts will provide some 2700 calories for the same weight, and almonds, cashews and brazils much the same. Barcelona nuts top 3000 calories to the pound. Those who believe it does something for their masculine image to boast of putting away a pound of steak at a sitting would have more to brag about if they had managed to get round a pound of peanuts. According to the National Academy of Sciences' list of recommended dietary allowances, whose statistics were not intended for Peruvian peasants, they would have consumed enough calories to keep a full-grown American male on the go for a whole day, having swallowed 300 grams of fat, enough protein for two days, and over 800 grams of carbohydrates. A pound of pecans would give them even more calories and fat, but a saner quantity of protein and some 600 i.u. of vitamin A against the paltry 80 offered in a pound of lean sirloin. Other and more serious comparisons could be made, all pointing to the indisputable superiority, in a balanced diet, of nuts over animal flesh.

The fact of the matter is that nuts are an excellent source of nutrition and one that has been almost totally disregarded in a society determined to centre its eating on meat rather than on the foods for which our species is specifically constructed and chemically attuned. Nuts more than almost any other made-for-man as distinct from man-made food put the 5 pounds-of-lentil-porridge school to flight, their high nutritive value making it unnecessary that they be eaten in such large quantities as the watery meats.

Beans and the pulses, hardly less neglected in the West, also help greatly to achieve an easier and more natural balance of nutrients, reducing the total food intake with all the extra mental and physical alertness this invariably brings. Whatever way one cuts the cake, the answer remains the same – there is no valid reason for claiming superiority for meat over a vegetarian diet. Even if dairy products are excluded, plant foods can and should supply our species with everything that it needs. As nutritionists such as Dr Frey Ellis and Prof J. W. T. Dickerson have made abundantly clear, plant foods are not only absurdly undervalued for their nutritional worth, but if fed directly to man rather than after processing through animals they can increase the nutritive yield per acre by up to ten fold. Soya beans, for example, yield seven times as much amino acid per acre as milk production and eight times as much as egg production. An animal must consume seven plant calories in order to produce one calorie's worth of human food . . .

The only reservation one must make about the completeness and adequacy of a fleshless diet, apart from the question of sufficient vitamin B12 for strict vegans under civilised conditions (see Chapter 7), is that freshness of food is always important, whether it is of plant or animal origin, and allowance must be made for this when comparing the needs of urban man with the requirements of those fortunate enough to have access to food at the point of growth and time of harvest.

PROTEIN
More popular myths have been built around food than around almost any other aspect of our daily lives, and probably more nonsense has been talked about protein than any other nutrient. It has received a disproportionate amount of attention and reverence, and it therefore takes an undue amount of space to redress the balance.

For many years proteins were misleadingly classified as either 'first-class' or 'second-class'. The 'first-class' proteins were identified as being in the animal foods (meat, eggs and dairy products), while the 'second-class' were those found in plant life. Having helped to vilify and misrepresent the argument for a more natural and healthful eating pattern, the 'first- and second-class' classification has at last been abandoned. In its place there is now a concern to establish how useful a particular protein is to the body, and to express its 'utilisation' on a numerical scale.

Nutritionally proteins are assessed according to the amount of each essential amino acid they contain, and that amino acid which falls furthest below the standard of reference protein is said to be the limiting amino for the protein in question. For instance, the limiting amino acid in wheat and millet is lysine, and that in beans is methionine. If the diet contains both wheat (e.g., in bread) and beans, and provided enough of these is taken at the same meal, protein requirement will have been satisfied, a better quality protein meal having been obtained than from either eaten by itself. From a nutritional point of view animal or vegetable protein should not be differentiated. A protein that contains all the essential amino acids in suitable proportions has a high biological value and so is a high quality or 'complete' protein. Meat, dairy products, whole wheat, most beans and other plant forms, are complete proteins.

But this new method of assessment is still slanted by some in favour of animal foods (though no longer by the suggestion, now seen as untenable, that plant foods are inadequate), in that eggs may be chosen as the ideal reference protein. An odd choice at a time when there is wide doubt of the wisdom of including eggs at all in the adequate human diet, especially for men, in view of their high cholesterol level (*Mind and Body*, p. 1030, vol. 3, Orbis 1971).

If one accepts this point of reference it gives values in the 60–80 range for animal proteins, and a figure of mostly under 50 for plant proteins. But the point to note is that values are now based on the *proportions* of essential and non-essential amino acids and no longer on the misleading basis of 'first' or 'second' class.[2] The ten essential amino acids are threonine, valine, methionine, isoleucine, leucine, phenylalanine, tryptophan, lysine and (in childhood) histidine and arginine, and these have to be supplied in our food. Our bodies are able to manufacture the non-essential acids. As proteins are now judged on their individual merits instead of being lumped together, if one plant protein that is short of essential amino acid 'A', but has plenty of 'B' and enough of the others, is added to another that has adequate 'A' but less of 'B', together they make a total protein meal that is just as good as one of 'first-class' protein.

This principle of mixing complementary plant proteins is employed to create nutritious and inexpensive protein foods for undeveloped countries, and it also explains why a normal vegetarian diet supplies enough nourishment. The supplementary value (the *mixture*) of cereals and nuts is why the now popular *muesli* breakfast foods are so extraordinarily sustaining for the small amount that is needed. This more realistic and certainly more scientific method of valuing proteins has done much to bring greater recognition of the importance of plant foods. It has strengthened our realisation, so long buried by the prejudice of habit and its concomitant influence on both professional and lay opinion, that man does not need to eat any animal products whatsoever; so long, that is, that what is eaten is reasonably balanced and wholesome.

The new method of evaluating proteins has also enabled us to consider certain forms of food, long hallowed by greed and such irrelevancies as status-symbolism, on their own merits. Consider, for instance, that status-symbol of our time, so often quoted as a supreme source of nutrition, and for so long hard-sold by the massive American meat industry, the sacred beef-steak – about as high as you can go in flesh foods if it is protein you are after. As Table 3 shows, 100 grams (3½ ounces) of stewing steak has a protein content of about 29 per cent. But it also yields 14 grams of deeply suspect, high-cholesterol fat (and much more than 14 grams if you go for non-lean meat), up to 15 grams of saturated fatty acids, 59 per cent of dirty water, 242 calories, 5·0 mg of iron, 5·0 mg of vitamin B3, some other B-vitamins and negligible amounts of anything else worth having. Compare these figures with those for almonds, providing only about 5 per cent of water, 580 calories, a better quality protein, more but healthier fat, far less saturated fatty acids, and a much greater weight of the unsaturated. Almonds also give significantly larger quantities of iron, etc., and a soaring (even unnecessary) 247 mg of calcium against steak's eight.

Other and equally 'orthodox' authorities have shown a different approach to the relative nutritional merits of basic foods, but the inconsistencies are minor and almost always tending towards rather than away from the more balanced view this book is attempting to present. As an instance, in its section on protein *Mind and Body* (Part 95, 1972), apparently taking into account water content, shows thirteen sources of protein, giving a value of 10 to dried skim milk and moving down the scale to show sunflower seeds and peanuts at 8 apiece; cheddar cheese at 7·25; dried milk, green peas and haricot beans at 7; almonds at 6; beef at 4·80; evaporated milk at 2; fresh green peas at 1·60; and liquid milk at less than 1. Were the value of soya and wheat germ also acknowledged, they would top the list with ease.

In the protein stakes it is easy to see why the soya bean has been described as the most valued plant on earth. With its up-to-23 per cent of fat, not to mention vitamins A, B1 and B2, many vital trace elements, iron, calcium, phosphorus, a high calorie count, little or no starch, low carbohydrate content, and a rich source of the essential amino acid lysine (the main lack in bread, which otherwise can be a good source of balanced nutrients), there is little wonder that food technologists are giving it so much attention. Filling without fattening, it could be the answer not merely to a maiden's prayer, but also and more importantly to the needs of those two-thirds of the world's population known to be under-nourished. Its slight deficiency in the amino acid methionine can be overcome by blending it with other plant proteins, as already indicated, and fortification with cereal proteins will also increase the biological value to acceptable levels. Such supplementation is of course necessary with all foods, and no less so with meat. The amino acid minimum for adults, incidentally, can be obtained from a pint of soya bean milk or cow's milk and about four slices of bread each day.

The soya bean's main use at present is for high-protein food for livestock, but as mentioned in Chapter 2 its role in the shape of meat analogues and other forms of protein for human consumption is increasing rapidly as its value as a direct food for man is being recognised.[3]

It may surprise some readers to know that leaves are a further excellent source of protein. 'The nutritional value of leaf protein,' announced *The Lancet* (24.8.1968) '– better than most seed proteins and as good as many animal proteins – has been known for many years,' and in his paper 'Protein Metabolism' (*Proceedings of the Royal Society of Medicine*, vol. 60, November 1967) Dr N. W. Pirie has described how leaves, containing 15–25 per cent protein of good biological value, have been processed on a large scale at Rothamstead Experimental Station during the past twenty years. The ideal leaf-source is a by-product from some other crop, such as banana, jute, ramie, sugar-beet, sugar cane, sweet potato, or peas and beans harvested for canning or freezing. Such sources are at present largely wasted. 'Once the idea of using leaf protein as a human food is accepted it would, however, be reasonable to grow crops specially for this purpose because a greater yield of protein would be got from an acre in a year in this way than by conventional agriculture.' In a later paper, 'The Present Position of Research on the Use of Leaf Protein as a Human Food', Dr Pirie stated: 'Equipment has been designed with which 60–70 per cent of the protein can be extracted from various leafy crops . . . The product contains . . . 20–30 per cent of highly unsaturated fat. Human and animal feeding experiments show that it is better than other plant proteins.' (*Plant Foods for Human Nutrition*, vol. 1, no. 4, November 1969.)

In case it is suspected that food value calculations are being slanted by anxious governments in favour of plant foods because of recent realisation of the inevitability of population pressure and world resources compelling a reduction in stock farming, it may be of interest to note what an even older authority has had to say. The Medical Research Council's *Nutritive Values of Wartime Food* (HMSO) made it equally apparent that a mixed vegetarian diet will supply all the nutritive essentials. Their figures showed 16 per cent for sirloin, 14 per cent for steak, 17 per cent for stewing steak, 18 per cent for carcass veal and 25 per cent for corned beef. In this table fish boasts as high a protein content as sirloin, with cod, sole, salmon, crab and kipper at 16, 16, 17, 20 and 19 per cent respectively. Fresh eggs rate only 12·5 per cent, though the dried egg of wartime beat all rivals listed at 45·8 per cent, yeast food at 43·1 per cent being a close runner-up. Contrary to popular belief, fish and eggs do not make large contributions to most nutrients, thought they are useful sources of vitamin D.

Unsurprisingly (at least to the higher primates and vegetarian man), then as now it was acknowledged that it is the nuts and pulses that present the greatest challenge to the over-stated claims for the virtues of animal foods – though the wider use and availability of cereal crops keep the grain foods highest of all plant protein sources at the present time. Haricots at 21·4 per cent, lentils at 23·8 per cent (some at 29 per cent), dried peas at 24·5 per cent, almonds at 20·5 per cent, peanuts at 28·1 per cent, soya at 40·4 per cent – even thirty years ago these percentages allowed no justification for the traditional belief in the superiority of flesh foods.

What is more important than the reduced significance of meat is this now more widely acknowledged value of the plant alternatives. In his paper 'Proteins', Dr F. Wokes has written:

Although animal foods are generally considered to be richer sources of protein, various plant foods such as nuts and pulses have a higher protein content than meat, milk or eggs calculated either on their composition as prepared for cooking or eating, or on the calorie basis. Deficiency of some essential amino acids such as lysine or methionine in individual plant proteins can be largely overcome by blending different plant proteins producing mixtures with biological values perhaps 15–25 per cent below those of human milk protein. (*Plant Foods for Human Nutrition*, vol. 1, no. 1, May 1968.)

Great Britain even more than America has lagged way behind the rest of the world in appreciating the range, uses and food value of nuts and the pulses. On the continent of Europe, particularly in Greece, and in India and most Asian countries, their nutritive value is well known and utilised. They are one of the most economical and accessible forms of protein. Little used in the UK except when tinned and covered in ketchup, the haricot bean has many uses, as has the valuable and similarly neglected butter bean. But delicatessen and health food shops can usually offer such changes – well-known already in the USA – as the red kidney, pinto, aduki, gram, dhal, cannellini, black-eyed, and ceci beans. Beans, in short, greatly widen the culinary horizons of anyone wishing to subsist pleasurably on plant foods. The appreciable quantities and quality of protein in the common pulses, together with other foods, supply the range of amino acids necessary for health.[4] Sprouted dried beans, the shoots being delicious, are another valuable source of nourishment.

But it cannot be over-emphasised that, taken all in all, the most overlooked and valuable source of protein and most of the other nutrients essential to man is to be found in nuts. Highly nutritious, their value has quite simply been neglected in favour of meat products for the richer countries and cereals for the poorer. In an address to the Northern Nut Growers' Association at Stamford, Connecticut, as far back as 1917, Dr John Harvey Kellogg pointed out that one pound of walnut meats has the equivalent food value of four pounds of red meat or ten pounds of chicken broilers, or $9\frac{1}{2}$ pounds of milk or 22 pounds of lobster. For sheer food value, a 126 g cup of walnuts producing 790 calories and 26 g protein may be compared with a 224 g cup of cow's milk producing 160 calories and 9 g protein. (NVF). An acre of walnuts will supply more than 1000 pounds of shelled meats with a food value of 3,000,000 calories. This is twenty times the amount that the same acre would yield in beef. The protein quantity of the nuts would be as great as in beef and of superior quality. It is to man's shame that these values in nuts and the pulses have been ignored for so long by those whose eating pattern has been under the thumb of the powerful meat industry and Western man's acquired preference for animal flesh. Here, as Kellogg said, '. . . is a veritable treasure of wealth, a potential food supply which may save the world from any suggestion of hunger for centuries to come if properly utilised . . . The nut should no longer be considered a table luxury. It should become a staple article of food and may most profitably replace the pork and meats of various sorts which are inferior foods and recognised as prolific sources of disease.'

His words are even more applicable today than they were in 1917, but as Professor Henry Bailey Stevens has pointed out, the inertia against change has been tremendous. Producers trained in the skills of their commodity and involved with heavy capital investments, look for more of their own kind of business, not for less or for diversification. Commodity organisations intensify such a viewpoint and can turn definite pressures against changes in the status quo. Processors, distributors and financial interests reflect a similar attitude. The most likely factors to bring about the change-over are the soaring cost of animal products, and a hungry world demanding that the affluent nations should recognise the ecological priority of a generally accepted (and, as it happens, more humane) diet.

Should I seem to have strayed a little from the point, these asides relate as much to protein as to any other constituent. No vegan should lack protein in view of the high concentrations in nuts, soya beans, cereals, whole grains, dried peas and beans, brewers' yeast, sunflower seeds, sesame seeds, wheat germ, avocados, and plant milk; and the lacto-vegetarian's acceptance of cow's milk, cheese and eggs on top of all the other protein sources available to him increases the absurdity of any suggestion that a diet merely excluding actual flesh could be in any way inadequate.

As is widely acknowledged, it is all too easy in the West to eat too much rather than too little. If we eat something of poor protein content but high calorific value, we may well be absorbing more calories than we need without obtaining enough protein. Hence the importance of understanding the balances involved – whether one eats meat or not. However, the danger is not great, and in the developed countries most of us eat more than we need.[5]

This section might best be rounded off by considering just what protein is in fact obtained from a modest vegan or lacto-vegetarian diet for a single day. Calories must be taken into account at the same time because of their inter-relationship. The following is not being suggested as a necessarily perfect or exciting menu, but as an example of a very simple meal pattern for one day only. The first of the two columns of figures on the right represents grams of protein, the second column calories. Authorities differ slightly in their recommended daily dietary allowance of proteins and calories, but for the purposes of this sample we can take the needs of a grown man aged 22–35 as being roughly 2800 calories and 65 g protein. Some authorities have suggested a protein intake of 1 g per kg body weight (hence 70 g protein for the 'average' (?) man of 70 kg), but today it is considered that less than this is enough, provided some of the protein is of high quality. Proteins provide materials for growth and repair of body tissues; they can also give energy and convert into fat; and in thickening arteries and blood they slow down the physical and mental processes.

Breakfast:	2 slices wholewheat bread	6 :	120
	½ oz nut butter	4 :	90
Lunch:	4 oz potatoes	5 :	105
	3 oz green beans, etc.	4 :	60
	3 oz cheddar cheese *or* almonds	21 :	445
	Orange, banana, pear	3 :	265
Dinner:	½ lettuce	2 :	30
	1 tomato	2 :	40
	2 oz dried dates	5 :	160
	2 slices rye or pumpernickel bread	4 :	60
	½ oz cashew nut cream	3 :	60
	2 oz cheese *or* nuts	14 :	30
		71 :	1665

Not exactly a gourmand's idea of high living, yet giving more protein than is needed by a healthy, adult male. Such figures are difficult to relate to the popular concept of vegetarians as protein-deficient. The opposite seems to be the case. What is needed, in view of the fact that this day's menu in fact omits a number of items that would normally be added (plant or cow's milk, beans, yoghurt, eggs, additional salad vegetables, fruit juices, macaroni, rice, salad or cooking oils, beverages, perhaps the odd soup or apple pie), is some way of *reducing* the protein. The calories are obviously going to look after themselves. This reduction could be achieved by using butter or margarine instead of nut-based butters or cream. Where peanut butter supplies 4 g protein to the half-ounce, butter or margarine give only 1 g to 2 ounces. Alternatively, 2 ounces of cheese or nuts in place of 3 ounces would take off 7 g of protein. The ease with which the protein intake can be overdone is shown by the value of a cup of lentils – 20 g (twice as many as a cup of milk) – though admittedly a cup of cooked lentils is a fairly demanding way of getting nourishment that can more easily be obtained from other plant sources, as *Black's Medical Dictionary* obviously knew. Even an ounce of wheat germ sprinkled over an ounce of cornflakes at breakfast will supply a further 9 g of protein, and never mind the milk. Add an egg to the breakfast menu, as the lacto-vegetarian may wish to do, and a further 6 g of protein has been provided.

It can be seen, therefore, that those who eat a high proportion of meat and little else can more easily fall below the target of 2800 calories. To get this number would mean eating over 3 pounds of lean steak every day, which would be far less beneficial than achieving the same calorie count by eating nearly a pound of walnuts – though neither is recommended. Far better to step up the calorie intake, although few of us lack carbohydrates unless our diets are hopelessly inadequate or unbalanced; if the calories are adequate, protein needs will be satisfied.

CARBOHYDRATES

Where proteins are primarily useful to build the body and repair the tissues, carbohydrates provide us with the heat and energy we need to function each day. They have provided a large part of the calorie count of our diet ever since cereals became of major importance. The principal sources are best found in whole grain cereals, breads, cornmeal, potatoes, macaroni products, dried beans and roasted nuts. Unfortunately all too many of us instead of recognising the value of such sources as barley, rye, buckwheat and brown rice, get a lot of our carbohydrates from such substances as sugar and its many products, and from those cakes, biscuits and so forth which are usually made from refined flours and have rightly been condemned by all nutritionists. Writers of the calibre of Doris Grant and John Yudkin have said most of what needs to be said on this subject, and it is beyond my brief to go into too many details, but it is the starchy staple foods such as bread and potatoes that supply us with many important vitamins, minerals and substantial amounts of protein as well, and these tend to be blamed too readily for obesity. It is true that fat is laid down in the body if more starch food is eaten than is necessary for the energy expended, and it is also true that refining of grains and their products is partly responsible for obesity (because the bran and other nutrients that help the digestion and use of starch are removed), but obesity is brought about chiefly by the total intake of calories being more than we need. As our diet consists of about 40 per cent fat (an excessive amount in the view of some authorities), 12 per cent protein and less than 50 per cent carbohydrate (against a carbohydrate intake of up to 80 per cent starch in some less developed countries) quite clearly the omnivorous 'fatties' in our midst would be hard put to it to suggest that starches alone have expanded their waistlines. No dietary standard for carbohydrates has in fact been properly established, as the body can get along very well with far less than most of us take in. Perhaps the most unnecessary source of all is white sugar, which is 100 per cent carbohydrate and robs the body of calcium in the process of being converted into heat. 'Eat less and exercise more' is for most of us the best answer to any anxiety about carbohydrates' place in our lives. As J. W. Lucas of the Radiation Protection Service, Manchester University Institute of Science and Technology, has said, most foods contain a number of energy sources although one particular source may predominate; the energy value of a foodstuff can be calculated if its composition has been determined, and some examples are on the following page.

FATS

Fats also produce heat and energy, offering in addition protection from injury to the kidneys and other organs, and they store long-term energy in various parts of our bodies.

The preferable sources of fat include such vegetable oils as sunflower, soya bean, corn, peanut, cottonseed and olive; nuts, avocados, margarine and various seeds; and eggs and dairy products for those not wishing to exclude animal sources.

The dangers inherent in animal fats, so high in saturated fatty acids, have been discussed exhaustively; as most of us know, the discussion usually centres on the rôle of saturated versus unsaturated fats. There is no question but that animal fats (including dairy products and eggs) contain cholesterol, and it is now generally accepted that an excess constitutes a danger to human health. Vegetable fats, on the other hand, consist mainly of what are called poly-unsaturated fats and contain no cholesterol. Instead the substances known as sitosterols are found, and these do not behave in the same way. Apart from containing unsaturated fatty acids, vegetable fats are more digestible than animal fats.

Food	Approx. Portion (oz)
Butter or margarine	½
Peanut butter	⅗ (tablespoon)
Cheese	⅘ (1 in. cube)
Sugar	1
Dry cereal flour	1
Prunes, dry, whole	1⅓
Bread	1⅓ (1⅔ av. slice)
Peas (shelled)	3½
Milk	5 (⅔ glass)
Banana	5 (1 medium)
Potato	5 (1 average)
Apple	6 (1 large)
Lean meat	2 (uncooked)
Lettuce	20

As a consequence, it is the belief of vegetarians and many nutritionists and medical people that we do best to use those fats which come from non-animal sources, but with the proviso that the greatest harm from both saturated and unsaturated fats comes when they are used as shortening or cooking oil – that is to say, when heated with other foods, in particular the starches. Almost no one today would defend, in an otherwise adequate diet, the consumption of cakes, pastries, fried bread or potatoes, pie crusts and the like, tempted though most of us are likely to be by such beguiling substances.

There is no official government minimum laid down for fat intake, but nutritionists have suggested that a fat consumption providing some 25 per cent to 30 per cent of the total calories may be compatible with good health. For those with a penchant for the often depressing evidence of statistics, the following list may be useful (Watts, B. K.; Merrill, A. L.; *Composition of Foods*, US Dept. of Agriculture, 1963):

Saturated and unsaturated fatty acids in foods per 100 grams (edible portion)

Food	Total grams saturated fatty acids	Total grams unsaturated fatty acids
Beef	12	12
Lamb	12	9
Pork	19	27
Cow's milk	15	10
Soya bean milk	3	15

Saturated and unsaturated fatty acids per 100 grams (edible portion)

	Total grams saturated fatty acids	Total grams unsaturated fatty acids
Cheese (cheddar)	18	12
(cream)	21	13
(cottage)	2	1
Chicken	2	3
Eggs (chickens')	4	6
Herring	2	2
Butter	46	29
Lard	38	56
Corn oil	10	81
Soya bean oil	15	72
Safflower oil	8	87
Shortening (animal and vegetable)	43	52
Shortening (vegetable)	23	72
Margarine	18–19	60–61
Olive oil	11	83
Cornmeal, white	Trace	3
Wheatgerm	2	8
Avocado pulp	3	9
Olives	2	16
Sesame seed (whole)	7	40
Soya beans (dry)	3	13
Almonds	4	47
Brazils	13	49
Coconut	30	2
Cashew	8	35
Peanut	10	34
Pecan	5	59
Walnut (black)	4	49

MINERALS

No sensible vegan or lacto-vegetarian diet is likely to lack in minerals, but it is relevant to consider the function and chief non-animal sources of some of these.

Iron. Iron helps resistance to disease, red blood-cell formation, the maintenance of a correct metabolism, and the supply of oxygen to the blood. It is found in whole seeds (wheat, oats, etc.), raisins, wheat germ, lentils, prunes, dates, apricots, spinach and other green leafy vegetables, dried beans, wholemeal bread, brewers' yeast. For ovo-lacto-vegetarians, eggs are a further source. Milk and cheese contain very little, and butter and cooking fats (animal and plant-derived) none at all. Men and women are said to need 10 and 18 mg respectively each day.

Sodium. Sodium plays a vital rôle in the body's metabolism and most foods contain it. Anyone who lacks it has gone very wrong somewhere, and four to five grams is the amount required daily by the average adult.

Calcium. Building bones and teeth, helping the blood to clot, and performing other useful functions that need bother the average vegetarian no more than the average omnivore, calcium accounts for around 1 kg of the human adult's body weight. Some 800 mg are needed daily. Meat and eggs are a poor source, and though cow's milk has 118 mg to 100 g, a higher figure is obtained from almonds (234), turnip greens (246) and other green vegetables. Cereal foods are a further useful source.

Phosphorus. Comprising some 1 per cent of our total body weight, phosphorus helps the kidneys, the bones, and all living and growing tissue. Deficiency is rare, phosphorus being found in all natural food. Vitamin D deficiency can prompt defects of phosphate metabolism, as can kidney disorders and other factors. Toasted whole wheat bread and cashew nuts are good sources, as is the ubiquitous soya bean (cooked), peanuts, cheese and to a lesser extent, eggs. Nuts, beans, leaf and root vegetables, dried fruit – these are all good sources. The Food and Nutrition Board of the American National Research Council recommends that phosphorus intake should be at least equal to that of calcium during childhood and the latter part of pregnancy and lactation. For the rest of the time we shouldn't need to give it a second thought.

Iodine. Again no problem. Fish are the main source, of course, but vegetables lead the rest of the field with 28·0 (average) micrograms to 100 g against eggs' 14·5, dairy products' 13·9, and bread and cereals' 10·5. We need about one microgram per kilogram of body weight, and any reasonable diet gives us plenty. Unsurprisingly, seaweed is a good source, also of many other minerals and trace elements including calcium, sodium, iron, copper, potash, nitrate, phosphate, chlorine, sulphur, etc. Carrageen and dillisk are two forms of edible seaweed that have been dried and eaten for many centuries, and seaweeds are also used as a general fertiliser and for feeding to animals. Seaweed appears to confer benefits all round, and while it may at present have little to do with the iodine intake of most of us, it may well be due for fresh prominence now that plant alternatives to meat are so much in vogue.

VITAMINS
Beef steak is 49 per cent water, 35 per cent fat, 15·5 per cent protein, and

about 0·2 per cent calcium, phosphate and other minerals. A total of 99·7 per cent. The remaining fraction is comprised of vitamins. Bread, with 34 per cent water, 55 per cent carbohydrates, 8 per cent protein and 0·8 per cent fat, reaches 99·8 per cent before we can consider the mineral and vitamin content.

Nevertheless, vitamins are extremely important. They make the food we eat usable to the body for its proper functioning; they are also essential to normal metabolism; they are present in most foods; and if we lack them we suffer from deficiency diseases. They fall into two categories – fat soluble and water soluble. The former dissolve easily in fat, the latter in water. It is important to avoid boiling the water containing water-soluble vitamins, as this will cause the food to lose its nutritional value.

Vitamin deficiency should not be found in sensible vegan, vegetarian or omnivorous diets, so their function and sources will be only briefly considered.

Vitamin A. Promoting growth, skin health, and contributing to the well-being of the respiratory area of the body, vitamin A comprises a group of fat-soluble compounds and is present in liver, some dairy products, vegetables and dried fruits in considerable quantities. 100 grams of raw carrots give 11,000 international units, 100 g of butter 3,300. Two ounces of fried beef liver will give you 30,280 and a cup of dried apricots 16,350, but as the day's average is 750μg retinol equivalents for a normal adult, no sleepless nights need be spent worrying about whether one is getting enough. However, as steak gives only about 15 units to 3 ounces, and milk only 350 to a cup, the avid flesh-eater must be careful to eat enough of those plant foods that supply this vitamin. Equally, the health-addict must be careful. In 1974 a Surrey man, reputedly a scientific adviser, ate an excessive number of vitamin A tablets and died as a result. The newspapers reported that he drank himself to death on carrot juice, but in fact the vitamin A in vegetables occurs as carotenes which the body converts into a controlled supply of the vitamin.

But excess and deficiency are both rare, though it should be remembered by flesh-eaters that there is more vitamin A in the fat of free-range animals than in many stall-fed and 'factory-farmed' beasts and birds, so milk and eggs may be a good or bad source according to the feeding methods employed.

The B vitamins. Water soluble, these are very important. For proper digestion, the efficient use of fuel foods, the breaking down of proteins, for body growth and the proper maintenance of the nervous system, the B's are essential. They lose their potency through prolonged soaking or boiling, so the water used in cooking should be utilised for stock, etc., if the maximum value is to be derived. They must be taken in proportionate amounts. For example, a person who consumes a minimum amount of vitamin B1 must have a comparable intake of B6 in order to avoid any deficiency.

B1 (Thiamin). The amount needed is in ratio to body weight, physical activity and metabolic weight, but chiefly to the intake of carbohydrate. Under normal conditions 1·2 mg are enough. But as B-group vitamins are synthesised by bowel bacteria, an antibiotic can kill the bacteria and produce a deficiency in what is apparently an adequate diet. Hence the frequent prescription of vitamin B alongside a course of oral antibiotics. Muscle tenderness, constipation, irritability and heart irregularities are among the signs of thiamin deficiency, and of course beri-beri. The best sources of thiamin are yeast, the bran and germ of cereals, pulses, beer, and to a lesser extent vegetables, meat and milk. White flours often have synthetic thiamin added to compensate for the removal of the wheat germ and bran in milling.

B2 (Riboflavin). The energy chain processes depend upon this vitamin which, like Thiamin, is derived in large quantities from yeast, but is also found in wheat germ, wholemeal flour, almonds, eggs, milk and dairy products, offal and most other foods. Cooking and heat do not harm this vitamin, and with about 1·7 mg needed daily by the adult male there is no real excuse for being deficient in it. If one is, a dry skin and cracks in the corners of the mouth may be warning signs.

B3 (Niacin). Niacin, nicotinic acid or nicotinamide is also necessary to produce energy. Deficiency leads to metabolic disturbances, especially to the nervous system. Pellagra is the chief niacin-deficiency disease. Nuts, dried fruit, grain products and various other foods produce good amounts of niacin, but once again brewers' yeast and wholewheat flour are particularly good sources. 18 mg is considered adequate for an adult male, and as it is manufactured in the body from the amino acid tryptophan, a diet including adequate protein increases the total intake of niacin equivalents and makes deficiency unlikely in most Western diets.

B6 (Pyridoxine). Apart from those dealt with above, three other vitamins of the B complex which contribute to forming the co-enzymes necessary for release of energy from fats, proteins and carbohydrates, are considered by most authorities. These are pyridoxine, pantothenic acid and biotin. Pyridoxine is widely available in vegetable foods (particularly cereals and the pulses), and animal sources. Panthothenic acid is also very plentiful. Biotin is a growth factor for many plants and animals and is found in yeasts, liver, etc., and can be made by the bacteria in the human intestine. We need about 2000 mg of B6 daily, and while not everyone wants yeast every day, any more than they do liver, there is plenty in wheat germ, wholewheat bread, corn, cabbage and bananas, though very little in milk and eggs.

B12 (*Cyanocobalamin*). This vitamin is of little consequence in a lacto-vegetarian diet, and today even orthodox opinion appears to be divided as to whether vegans need to worry. However, deficiency does occur, not merely in some vegans, but even more widely among flesh-eaters. No official minimum requirement appears to have been decided upon, though between 3 and 5 micrograms have been suggested. Deficiency can lead to pernicious anaemia and nervous disorders. Non-flesh sources have been listed as brewers' yeast, soya bean milk, wheat germ, sea kelp, eggs, dairy products and various prepared foods in which it is an additive. The Vegan Society was for long very sensitive to accusations that a diet excluding all animal products might produce B12 deficiency symptoms, and in their published literature they have considered the matter at some length. This is reviewed in Chapter 7.

Folic acid has to be considered alongside B12, and both will cure anaemia (though folic acid has to be administered *with* B12 in any such treatment). Folic acid is available in all fresh vegetables and in liver, the daily need being around 200 mg. The other members of the vitamin B complex are considered of doubtful value or rarely lacking. These are inositol, choline, para-aminobenzoic acid, citrovorum, B13 and B14.

Vitamin C (*Ascorbic acid*). The best sources of this water-soluble vitamin are fruit and fresh vegetables, but it is destroyed by drying and cooking, though to a lesser extent in acid-containing foods such as tomatoes. 30 mg (NVF say 60 mg) are necessary for an adult male, and this is provided by an orange, or a helping of broccoli or sprouts, or a few tomatoes, or just any normal, sensible diet. It may help to prevent colds and is frequently deficient in elderly people who confine their diet to little but bread and tea. Vitamin C is not needed by carnivorous animals, and most omnivores and many plant-eating animals get by on a quarter or less of what our own species requires. Our need to consume the fruit and other plant life that gives us this vitamin, and to do so daily (for our bodies cannot store it), is one of the indications that man is naturally frugivorous.

Vitamin D (*Cholecalciferol*). Like vitamin A, this is fat-soluble, and the best sources are direct sunlight, eggs, milk and butter. In its synthetic form it is widely added to such foods as margarine, but in fact most of us are independent of dietary supplies because we absorb it automatically when sunlight falls on our skins. It is the only vitamin that humans can synthesise for themselves – if they live in a good climate.

Vitamin E (*Tocopherol*). Another fat-soluble vitamin, of which we need some 20 mg daily if we are not to run the slight risk of premature birth and sterility. But it is not thought that humans run much risk of deficiency, and the population graph suggests our species may be getting rather too much. It comes in such extremes as egg yolk and lettuce, as well as from such sources as wheat embryo, milk fat and oats. Vegetable oils provide plenty, and six tablespoons of medicinal wheat germ oil would be enough for a small army.

Vitamin K (*Menaphthone*). This is a further fat-soluble vitamin needed for the clotting of blood. Most green plants and some fruits contain it and are the best sources. Lucerne (alfalfa) and spinach are particularly rich in vitamin K, though an up-to-date Popeye might equally well get his quota from the soya bean.

As the more responsible authorities make plain, only those whose diet is improperly balanced need worry about their vitamins. Babies on cow's milk may need vitamins A, C and D, however, as may some elderly people who are not looking after themselves properly. It is also acknowledged that those who subscribe to the 'whole food' philosophy have scientific fact on their side, for the sort of diet they advocate is undoubtedly richer in vitamins than are the highly processed and sophisticated mass-produced foods. Instant potato, for example, has recently been found to lack the vitamin C which is present in the original article. But because of the improbability of any reasonable diet providing too few vitamins, further discussion is best left to those writers whose concern is with the broader issues of nutrition.

Nevertheless, a little knowledge about nutrition – as distinct from a lot of worry, prejudice and superstition – is no bad thing, particularly for any minority subject to the baiting and half-knowledge of those for whom majority rule and conformity provide an often false sense of security. For fallacies about food are thick on the ground. As common as the erroneous belief that vegetarians don't get enough protein is the notion that butter and lard contain it, or that cow's milk supplies iron or is a perfect food.[6] Most of the illusions seems to have been designed to support the habit of eating meat and animal products, and it comes as a surprise to many to learn that bread and cereals supply as much protein in the average Englishman's diet as does his meat.

Another fallacy that needs to be got into perspective is that the many miserably malnourished people who are to be seen in such countries as India are evidence of the inefficacy of a vegetarian diet. But the people of India – where the main dietary deficiencies are in calories, protein, calcium, vitamin A and riboflavin – are largely vegetarian because they ran out of land two or three thousand years ago, for even then India was densely populated. They had no land to spare for the luxury of meat. Their religious leaders forbade animal food, with the exception of cow's milk, for this is the most economical food of animal origin even though it needs some six to eight times more land than for bread. So the vegetarians of the East were largely compelled by economic necessity, and the superficial observer may well look at the malnourished and crippled bodies of children and adults and conclude that so pitiful a scene is evidence of the foolhardiness of cutting out animal products.

There is no doubt that starving people who add some animal food to their diet, whether milk, fish or meat, are physically better off, but although a measure of animal food must of course make a poor diet more satisfactory, this is no evidence for animal food being natural to humans. Adding meat and dairy products to a poor vegetarian diet is one way of coping with the deficiency (if someone is willing to import these expensive products), but a far better way, as is now being widely realised, is to ensure instead that starving people get more of the essential proteins and vitamins from the leafy vegetables, roots, nuts and fruit to which their bodies are naturally receptive, and which give the highest yields per acre of calories, protein and other nutrients, and less of those starchy roots or cereals (so often refined at that) which tend to provide the bulk of the diet.

As F. A. Wilson has explained so clearly, the industrial West has not only inflicted on *itself* the refined and devitalised foods that have done so much harm. Where 'civilisation' has spread, the refinery and the mill have gone too. And because the colonial people and the vast hordes of the East were already poorly fed before the white man came, his advent has meant a degree of malnutrition far worse than in the West. India, Malaya and China knew no rice mills until the Europeans came. Each Indian family had its equivalent of a pestle and mortar of wood, in which the rice was pounded and the husks broken. Then the rice was shaken in the wind on a shallow wicker trough and the husks blown away. Some of the bran also went with the wind, but enough remained to give the rice a distinctly brown colour, and much germ remained attached to the rice grains.

Then the rice mills and the profit-seekers came along, and rice-growing became an industry. Every bit of bran was removed and not a speck of germ remained in the starch-filled white grains. As usual, the best part went to the fortunate animals. Talc was often rubbed on to the grains to make them whiter still. As with whole and refined wheat, refined rice compares very badly with its home-pounded equivalent, known as 'paddy'. Paddy contains 13 per cent more protein, and the best part of it; three times more calcium and phosphorus, twice as much iron, ninety times more vitamin A, eight times more vitamin B1, ten times more vitamin B2, and nearly three times more nicotinic acid. Bad as is the average European diet, the average oriental diet is roughly three times as bad. On his diet of refined rice the Indian gets less than a fifth as much vitamin B1, and less than an eighth as much vitamin A as the European. It is hardly surprising that deficiency diseases like beri-beri, and blindness, are so common.

It is necessary not only to show why meat and animal products are un-necessary to the human constitution, but to underline that we cannot take it for granted that our natural food is almost anything that is not derived from animals. Science and technology have helped to create such an arti-ficial and greed-controlled environment that even our daily bread (if that is what we should term those flabby slabs of chalk-white pap, steam-baked pre-sliced, and tasteless) owes more to the chemist's laboratory than to a field of golden corn. Man-cursed, the sign of bad bread is that it has to be advertised on television.

But flesh-eating is the practice on which this book is centred, and so far from it being possible to make out a sound general defence of the habit of eating pieces of animals, or their surplus fluids and menstrual discharge (which is precisely what we are doing every time we tuck into a steak, a glass of milk or an egg), the dangers in so doing are probably greater than anything but a singularly unbalanced plant-diet. Once we can accept this fact, and have absorbed the 'basics' of nutrition and our physiology, we should not find it difficult to settle into a dietary routine that is free of daily concern about precisely how many grams or units of this or that we are pushing down our throats. Eating and drinking can and should be a simple pleasure, given its due place and attention. Taken to excess, either in quan-tity or in the time we give to worrying or enthusing about it, it can lead to sickness or obsession. By all means let the whole man have whole (and humane) foods, but if he spends all his time thinking about them he may become a bore to his friends and forget about a lot of other things that are just as important and far more interesting. Balance in dealing with the subject of food is as necessary as the balance in what we actually eat.

But it would not show balanced judgement for the heavy meat-eater to depart over-night from the eating pattern of a lifetime. If a changeover is being considered, it would be unwise to switch immediately to a straight diet of raw vegetables. The bugs that we carry in our guts will not neces-sarily take kindly to too sudden a rejection of the meat and fish to which they have become accustomed. Their populations should be changed slowly from the putrefactive to the fermentive. Eating sour milk and plenty of fruits can help to make the transition, though merely cutting out all meat and retaining the intake of dairy products should bring nothing but benefit. Lacto-vegetarianism deprives the meat-eater of nothing his system should miss. Too sudden an alteration, however – from daily steaks to veganism, for instance – and your angry body will force your mind to cheat. Deprived too quickly of their animal products, your addicted cells will find a way of making you believe you can't do without them. Cut down on the meat and fish at once, and if at the same time you replace them with the right non-animal foods, any craving for flesh and even dairy products will peter out.

On a more natural diet you are quite likely to lose weight if, on the old diet, you were carrying around too much. This is nothing to worry about and everything to be thankful for. On a natural diet, very thin people, after losing some weight, usually begin to put it on and often find in time that they have approached a more normal weight. But it may take as much as a year or two, as weight increase is a slower business than weight reduction if excessive thinness was the result of glandular unbalance and the toxic properties of strong meats.

Children, whose lack of inclination to pounce upon the raw flesh that their mothers bring home from the shops should be evidence enough of its unsuitability, are usually more easily tempted to eat non-flesh foods than meat in any shape or form – even though family pressure has succeeded in making them accept it. The two meats to which many of us are most easily accustomed – chicken breast and bacon – are, unsurprisingly, the least representative of flesh food. The bland near-to-nothingness of the one, and the salty and more positive flavour of the other, neither of them reminding the consumer of blood and those strong juices that repel so many children – these have more affinity with non-flesh substances such as cereal products, yeast foods and appetizers like salted peanuts than with the coarse and acquired taste of rare steak and lamb chops.

Most children will, and should, eat many vegetables raw, and although the very young often make a fuss about eating the over-cooked vegetables that appear on so many dinner plates, they do not as a rule show any resistance to eating them before they reach the stove. Some raw vegetable foods should appear in most meals, with emphasis on salads and fruit. Raw grated vegetables and nuts can be sprinkled over cooked foods to encourage thorough chewing. There are endless variations of salads and raw vegetable dishes, and the bleak British salad of limp lettuce and an intrusion of tomato is a caricature for which no modern housewife has the slightest excuse except bone laziness or extra-culinary overwork. Herbs, preferably fresh, can add immeasurably to the pleasure of food, though no well run kitchen is without the biggest dried herb rack that money and space can afford. Pressure cookers and the 'Romatof' are wonderful devices for cooking vegetables, ensuring a degree of nourishment and flavour never experienced by those for whom a steaming saucepan is the normal cooking medium for vegetables.

This is not a cookery book, however; but to give a broad idea of the direction menus can take the following suggestions may be helpful.

Breakfasts are best based on fruits and that combination of cereals, nuts, dried fruit, etc., that is known on the continent as muesli and has become much more popular of late in prepared, packeted form, available under various brand names in virtually every grocers and supermarket. Wholemeal bread with the various nut butters, margarines, and such spreads as Barmene and Tartex, are extremely sustaining and very palatable.

After an adequate breakfast on such lines (and if you think cornflakes and bacon are more sustaining, you are the victim more of belief than of experience!), a light lunch in which salads and fruit predominate will keep both mind and body far more alert than those high-protein and stodgy meals with which too many of us end our useful work period before the day has got properly into its stride.

The main meal of the day should provide the bulk of the needed protein, and whether this is to be strictly vegetarian (in which case nuts, most legumes and grain foods provide what is needed) or lacto-vegetarian (the high protein content of most hard cheeses beats meat any time), the variety that may be introduced into such a diet usually astonishes those who previously believed that a meat-based diet gave greater choice. The opposite is the case, as any good vegetarian cookery book makes clear. In point of fact, many omnivorous diets are boring and monotonous in the extreme, and the unadventurous, 'typically English' meat-and-two-veg notion of culinary craftsmanship is surely the all-time nutritional low. There is something slightly pathetic about the ease with which many of us are conned by habit and the advertisers into believing that a portion of blanket-like factory-farmed chicken set off against a small pile of frozen peas and some over-boiled peeled potatoes, is hitting the double-top of *haute cuisine*.

Finally, and with no apology, I repeat that a balanced attitude to nutrition is what is needed. But do not be deluded by the sophistry of those who twist this to support the spurious nonsense of 'a little of what you fancy does you good'. A little of what we fancy may not do us so much harm that it should be avoided at all costs, but the fact remains that if what we are putting into our bodies is foreign to their chemistry, we are to that extent poisoning ourselves, whether what we fancy is the smoke of a single cigarette, a grain of arsenic or a lump of decomposing flesh. Balance in nutrition should be as between good and good, not good and bad. Balance for the human species is not eating flesh *and* plant life, but combining the various forms of the latter to create a balanced diet. Despite the many artifices, equivocations, back-pedallings and wishful thoughts with which most of us resist any pressure to do the thing that should come naturally and with the maximum benefit to ourselves as well as to the animals we exploit, it really is as easy as that. The proof, however, can only be in the eating.

Notes

1. Wide variations are available. 'Granogen' powdered soya milk contains 22·5 per cent protein (2·8 per cent for 1 to 7 dilution), 46·8 per cent carbohydrate (5·9 per cent), 22·6 per cent fat (2·8 per cent), 4·2 per cent ash (0·5 per cent), 3·9 per cent moisture (88·0 per cent), an ounce of the powder providing 136 calories and 100 i.u. of vitamin D. Whole dried cow's milk in the (MN) tables supplies 26·6 per cent protein, 37·6 per cent carbohydrate, 27·7 per cent fat, and approximately the same number of calories.

2. The idea that 'first-class' protein was found only in meat was knocked on the head in 1955 when *The Extra Pharmacopoeia* announced: 'The terms first and second class protein came into being in the first World War and were based on incomplete analyses of pure protein and on inadequate experiments on rats . . . the terms have now become meaningless and should be discarded.' Many other authorities have made similar statements (see *Mind and Body*, vol. 6, p. 2277; Davidson, *The Principles and Practice of Medicine*, p. 413, Livingstone, 1963).

   The capacity of proteins of different origin to make good one another's deficiencies when they are consumed together is known as their *supplementary value*.

3. Kitchen-garden enthusiasts can now grow soya beans successfully in Great Britain. The variety Fiskeby V Original, developed by Sven Holmberg in Sweden, can be raised in the south and south-east of that country, and should prove to be satisfactory in northern Europe. Seed is obtainable from Thompson & Morgan, the Ipswich seedsmen. North America, producing over three-quarters of the world's supply grown for animal feeds, has no problem – the Middle West is on the same latitude as Manchuria, the birthplace of the soya bean. Sown in mid-May in Britain it can be cropped green (to be eaten like runner beans) during August, or shucked for dried beans by the end of September. For those who wish to get the flavour and texture of meat without condoning the cruelty and health hazards that go with it, Courtauld's 'Vegex' is a meat analogue derived from soya or field beans with added vegetable (typically palm) oil, containing a negligible amount of cholesterol, and is one of several available brands that in most cases can fool the most dyed-in-the-wool flesh-addict. Other brands include Direct Foods' 'Protoveg' (containing vitamin B12), Granose's 'Soyapro', Itona's 'TVP', Mapleton's 'Maplemince', Marigold's 'Basic Protein', and 'Vitpro'; Courtauld's 'Kesp' contains 1 per cent of animal fat. In general the beef, bacon and ham flavours are the most convincing. 'Chicken' is still proving difficult. Chile has just built a multi-million pound plant to produce a soya and vegetable 'beefsteak' that should cost the housewife an eighth of what she pays for the second-hand commodity. In pet foods, of course, TVPs have already gained a firm foothold and can entirely replace real meat for dogs and cats – at a consequent cost saving. Purina 'Dog Chow' and Spratts 'Dog Diet' are two varieties widely available. Although Fiskeby V Original is related to the soya bean, its suppliers stress it should not be confused with field beans (*vicia faba*), which are still primarily an animal feed. Low in carbohydrate, yet high in calories, Fiskeby V Original is approximately 40 per cent protein and an excellent source of vitamins A, B1, C and G; also of calcium, iron and phosphorus. Its small starch content has commended it to diabetics. It is interesting to compare the green bean with its 'textured' relative. Courtauld's 'Vegex', based on soya protein isolate, shows the following breakdown in a cup weighing 96 grams (net, dry): Water 3 per cent, calories 586, protein 45 g, fat 42 g, saturated acids 47 per cent, oleic acid 43 per cent, linoleic acid 10 per cent, carbohydrate 3 g, calcium 12 mg, iron 8 mg, nicotinic acid equivalent 6 mg. The figures for calcium and iron were not obtained on 'Vegex'

itself, but are typical of other products based on soya bean isolate. No vitamin A, thiamin, riboflavin or ascorbic acid is present in 'Vegex'. For calorie-watchers, 'Protoveg' supplies less than half the calorific value shown in Courtauld's analysis, somewhat more protein (52 per cent), 1 per cent fat, and only ·2 per cent saturated fatty acids. The 47 per cent saturated fatty acids shown by Courtaulds is of course linked to the high fat content, which in turn helps to account for the additional calories. Although the 'Protoveg' analysis shows 31·5 per cent carbohydrates against Courtauld's 3 per cent, the greater proportion of the carbohydrates in 'Protoveg' are non-metabolisible. These comparisons show that the meat analogues offer a wide choice in nutritive balance. Which is as it should be.

4. 'Gelatin and certain vegetable proteins are deficient in some of the essential amino acids; but a mixed vegetable diet, including pulses, can supply enough of all.' Davidson, *The Principles and Practice of Medicine*, 6th ed., p. 413.

5. After stating that a 70 kg man can maintain nitrogen equilibrium on 32 g protein per day, D. S. Miller has said: '. . . the vulnerable groups in society are the toddlers and the lactating mother. Adult man can indeed live on bread alone, and protein-rich foods should be directed towards his wife and children.' *Proc. R. Soc. Med.*, vol. 60, Nov. 1967.

Experiments on university athletes and men in the United States Army have shown that an actual reduction in protein intake results in a marked improvement of physical performance. This contrasts sharply with the long-held idea that athletes need vast quantities of meat. Many athletic records have been held by vegetarians, including Olympic medals being won for running, swimming, etc. See Rudd: *Why Kill for Food?* et al.

6. Cow's milk contains almost no iron and would cause anaemia as a sole diet. It is almost completely lacking in vitamin C. It has value for infants and children lacking anything better, but adult men can obtain too much of the wrong kind of fat from it.

Seven

The Further Step

A vegetarian diet is the acid test of humanitarianism.
Leo Tolstoy

The unlimited capacity of the plant world to sustain man at his highest is a region yet unexplored by modern science ... I submit that scientists have not yet explored the hidden possibilities of the innumerable seeds, leaves and fruits for giving the fullest possible nutrition to mankind.
Mahatma Gandhi, quoted by Tendulkar, 1944

The rôle of plant foods relative to that of animal foods in human nutrition is one of the most crucial questions ... plants have constituted and will constitute the major part of the daily food of the developing countries, contributing as they do nine tenths of their calorie and protein supply.
Dr Boerma, director-general FAO,
Plant Foods for Human Nutrition, May 1968

Flesh eating is not necessary to health.
Encyclopaedia Britannica, 1973

THROUGHOUT the history of mankind, or at least since the agricultural revolution, the vast majority of our species has lived on little but grain. It seems absurd, therefore, that so many of us should regard veganism – with the excellent variety of foods it can offer – as a daring departure from the norm. With domestic animals eating up to ten times as much of the Earth's primary plant food as humans (see Dr Norman Wright, Deputy General, FAO, 1961, *Can Hunger Be Averted?*), and the problems of malnourishment and actual starvation greater than ever before, a serious world-wide study of the principles and practicability of vegan nutrition would be a responsible and reasonable measure wholly in line with current awareness of mankind's predicament.

Nonetheless, for the majority of omnivorous Westerners it is enough to make the first move the adoption of a lacto-vegetarian diet, though we cannot for ever shut our eyes to the fact that the further step of veganism may well come from necessity if not from choice, for the simple reason that the meat and dairy industries are inseparably linked luxuries it is becoming increasingly difficult to afford.

106

The logic of the vegan case is absolute. No one – whether nutritionist, physician, sociologist or layman – can rebut the veganic argument in any important respect. Veganism is part of the most truly civilised concept of life of which the human mind has been capable. More than ordinary lacto-vegetarianism, veganism 'speaks to the condition' of our modern world. That only a minute number of Western people puts its principles into practice is evidence of nothing but our reluctance to break with habit and to put conscience before the undoubted social inconveniences of a pattern of life that is foreign to the bulk of the society in which we live.

The objections to veganism, then, are selfish rather than rational. It is only fair to a courageous minority to make this quite clear, and I can say this because I am myself one of the many who *know* better than they *do*. I am not yet a fully practising vegan, although I would like to be. The pressures on most of us not to go the whole way are tremendous and, in many a family, sadly divisive. There must be numerous vegetarians who, in doubt and with despondency, have compromised their principles for the sake of a quieter or more workable life, perhaps putting an outwardly more harmonious background for their children before the obligation they feel in their hearts they owe to the world outside the closed circle of family. Whether the tension that can result is any easier to cope with than the social sacrifices demanded by greater consistency is something that can only be answered individually.

At first sight there is little in the veganic argument that is different from that of the lacto-vegetarian's. Reverence for life, environmental responsibility, man's physical and spiritual development – vegans and vegetarians share these concerns with equal conviction. But it has to be said that vegans show a more logical and consistent approach because of their practical acceptance of the fact that we cannot consume eggs and dairy products without tacitly supporting the ceaseless cruelty that is no more removed from the production of milk, butter, cheese, eggs and the many foods in which they are used than it is from the actual pieces of flesh which are where the lacto-vegetarian draws his line.[1]

It is not possible, or at least not practicable, to produce milk and milk products without subjecting both cow and calf to the full range of procedures, culminating in slaughter, that govern the life of domesticated cattle. Cows have to be subjected to yearly pregnancies so that the milk, cheese and cream that form a substantial part of the diet of both lacto-vegetarians and meat-eaters may be produced. Many imagine that the cow is only relieved of her surplus milk after her calf has been satisfied, but hardly any cows in dairy herds are allowed to suckle their calves for more than three days if at all. Dairy calves are now nearly always reared by hand so that the milk which the cow provides can be sold. 'Separating the calf from the mother shortly after birth undoubtedly inflicts anguish on both. Cattle are highly intelligent, and attachment between the calf and the mother is particularly strong.' (*Report of the Brambell Committee*, HMSO, 1965.)

The calves, the inevitable by-product of the continual pregnancies that are necessary to keep a cow producing milk, have several possible fates. They may go to slaughter almost immediately, their few brief hours of life involving separation from their mother, transport in trucks to market, and further handling and movement before their butchers turn them into veal and ham pies and drain their stomachs of the rennet that is used to make most commercial cheeses.

If they go to a white veal unit they will spend the rest of their lives tethered in narrow crates, deprived of water except in the specially designed slop with which they are fed, kept short of iron (to produce the white meat that is the sign of anaemia demanded by the public for this vilely procured product), and given little if any of the roughage that their special digestive systems as ruminants require. Often reduced to eating their own hair and nibbling their crates, they are denied even the comfort of bedding because their craving for solid food would tempt them to eat it. Many emerge from their crates at the end of their fourteen weeks of existence suffering from stomach ulcers and abscesses, and too weak to stand in the slaughter-house lorries. 'Calves at large,' said the Brambell Report, 'are normally active and playful animals.' So are human children, given the chance. When we are as concerned for the 'battered babies' of other species as we are for our own, we shall have learned to substitute the logic of civilised mankind for the barbarous insensitivity of savages.

Some 80 per cent of the beef produced is a by-product of the dairy industry, and calves from beef herds often have a comparatively tolerable fate, being allowed to suck, to run with their dams and to graze in the fields until the time comes for the fattening pens and the slaughter-house, but the surplus calves from the dairy herds are frequently sent to market when a week old (or less) and bought for rearing in intensive beef units if not immediately slaughtered.

In these days of artificial insemination, few 'bobby' calves are reared as bulls, and for the exceptions life will be largely one of solitary confinement with interludes serving real or artificial cows and rubber tubes. If female, the calves may be thought suitable to rear as dairy cows, in which case they are removed as soon after birth as possible so that the cow 'may settle down again in the herd'. That is, she is granted the minimum time to get over the strain of her frustrated pregnancies so that her milk can as soon as possible go to produce the all-important profits. Fed on milk substitutes, the calves' development is encouraged so that at 18–24 months they can begin the cycle of continuous pregnancies.

As *The New Scientist* (13.1.1972) admits, 'The modern dairy cow leads a hell of a life. Each year she hopefully produces a calf which means that for nine months of the year she is pregnant. And for nine months of each year she is milked twice a day. For six months she is both pregnant and lactating.' Details of the ailments she can succumb to while meeting these demands make painful reading, as do the remedies employed. Giving birth is often a prolonged and painful business for the cow, to be rewarded only by separation from her baby. A cow often cries out and searches for its calf for days after it is taken away. When after years of exploitation her milk yield drops, she is sent to the slaughter-house before profit turns into loss. As worn-out cow's meat is not popular in Britain, countless thousands of animals have been sent abroad for slaughter. The hideous cruelty found in continental abattoirs is too well-known to need repeating here and has for some time been a target for those who don't wish to give up eating meat, but, conscience partly awakened, are able to deceive themselves and others that if only our animals don't get their throats cut by foreigners, everything will be seen to be for the best in the best of all possible worlds.

For some animals in some parts of the world the 'humane' killer is employed. But that is the most one can say. For countless millions of creatures every single day brings a brutal and painful death unrelieved by even token attempts to lessen their sufferings. Even where the humane killer is used, the attendant circumstances of often long-distance transport, rough handling, food withheld before slaughter, the terror of the waiting within the smell of blood suffered by many creatures, and the violence in their handling at the hands of men whose concern for the feelings of the over-familiar objects of their livelihoods has inevitably been eradicated – these are all factors inseparable from the whole brutal and squalid business.

As K. Jannaway has written (*What Happens to the Calf?* The Vegan Society): 'All this to produce food for humans that is not necessary! Human babies should have their mother's milk, and children and adults the solid food appropriate to their dentition and digestive systems. These can easily be selected from richly varied plant sources. For babies and children where necessary or desired, and for invalids or those who still like to take milk ... nutritious plant-milks are available ... The dairy industry is inseparable from the cruel exploitation and degradation of helpless, highly intelligent animals.'

Egg production is also unacceptable to vegans because it involves the virtually unavoidable necessity to slaughter the male birds and insufficiently productive hens. Modern techniques with their battery and broiler systems, unnatural feeding, selective breeding and perverse methods of laying stimulation constitute continual ruthless exploitation. The cruelty and carelessness in the slaughter of chickens whether at the hands of the back-yard neck-wringer or on the conveyor belts of slaughtering plants, is as well-known and as obvious as the absence of public concern. The majority of us is successful in forgetting or ignoring even the furthest extremes of brutality if the alternative is to give up the sacrosanct slices and by-products of animals that we insist upon consuming.

Though we may be far from seeing such a vision realised, it cannot be denied that the adoption of a vegan diet throughout the world would not only release the huge areas of land now being used for animal exploitation, but would involve the right care of the land and its best use to satisfy the real needs of man and other forms of life. However, this argument has already been explored, and while it is tempting to discuss other aspects of the vegan régime (which embraces clothing, cosmetics, sport, and those other spheres of daily life that involve the misuse of animals), such investigations must be left to those who wish to take the matter further.

Vitamin B12

The only serious criticism that has been made of veganism relates to possible deficiency in vitamin B12. In the present state of knowledge it is a little difficult to know just how much of the problem – if problem there be – to present in this context. Medical and nutritionists' opinions are far from unanimous and there are some puzzling contradictions. The matter has not been simplified by the realisation that B12 deficiency is even more prevalent among meat-eaters than among vegans. Some recent research, indeed, has prompted the suggestion that its rare incidence among vegans – as being *due* to their veganism – is in doubt. The medical dictionary *Mind and Body* has already been quoted on this point (see page 70, and study of the medical journals provides ample evidence of deficiency among those whose nutritional standards would seem to be adequate. 'Vitamin B12 deficiency is a commoner cause of mental illness among omnivores than is generally believed,' it was stated in a leading article in *The Lancet* (ii, 309, 1969), 'and screening of all psychiatric patients for pernicious anaemia associated with such deficiency has been advocated.'

Lack of vitamin B12, then, can cause illness and in rare cases even death. It should be understood, however, that the same can be said of other nutritional scarcities (and excesses) and that B12 deficiency does not necessarily indicate that the patient has failed to consume the quantity considered to be adequate. He can eat the vitamin without his body being able to utilise it. What causes this intestinal ineptitude is as much in doubt as are such basic data as the minimal daily amount of B12 required by the human body. In fairness to nutritional experts, however, B12 was isolated only as recently as 1948, which in biochemical terms is no great while ago.

It is interesting and possibly very relevant that lifelong vegans seldom suffer from B12 deficiency. Where deficiency has been established, it has been mostly in people who have switched, perhaps too abruptly, from a diet based on animal products. This has helped to prompt the suspicion that as children brought up from birth on a vegan diet are able to absorb the B12 made by the bacteria in their colons, it may be that the perversion of the body's chemistry through meat-eating has made it impossible for a small number of people to switch to the more natural vegan diet later in life without showing signs of B12 deficiency.[2]

This is not to say, of course, that symptoms due to inadequate *intake* of B12 are not to be found in malnourished people the world over, whether they are omnivorous or more selective in their eating habits. An inadequate diet will be deficient in a great many elements, whether or not meat is included. Although volumes have been written about B12, it is in our knowledge of man's adaptational abilities that we have far to go; the uncertainties surrounding a clearly inadequate intake (irrespective of absorptional capacity) are less in dispute.

It is known that the bacteria in the human colon synthesise B12, but that in most cases this is not available for absorption by the large intestine because the absorption takes place in the lower end of the ileum (or small intestine). This absorption depends upon the presence of the 'intrinsic factor', a protein-like substance produced in the stomach. In the case of pernicious anaemia, for instance, this intrinsic factor is absent. There is some evidence that the large intestine of vegans can absorb B12 (Ellis, F. R.; Wokes, F., 'Vitamin B12', *The Vegan*, Winter 1966/67) – a point that may well be given more prominence as research continues.

Another point that has received some attention and has tended to confuse the issue, at least for the layman, is that vegans are prone to 'abnormal' electroencephalograms. The reason for this is in doubt, but 'is almost certainly not related to vitamin B12 deficiency' (Ellis, F. R.; Montegriffo, V. M. E., 'The Health of Vegans', *Plant Foods for Human Nutrition*, vol. 2, no. 2, January 1971). However, disagreement and partial knowledge surround this finding, and in view of the link that some have suggested it might be reasonable for the intrepid layman to question the basic assumption of abnormality. For if that 'abnormality' is being judged by chemical differences from those who eat animal products, it seems logical to suppose that healthy (and so presumably fully adjusted) vegans' (and other higher primates'?) EEGs are normal, but that meat-eaters' are not. What is normality? A blood chemistry that is the result of centuries of persistent wrong feeding and unnatural living conditions, or the state of equilibrium for which our species was designed? The answer seems obvious, the question almost absurd, yet allopathic medicine itself is based on the appallingly unscientific absurdity of dosing the symptoms of our unnatural habits with poisons instead of promulgating the fundamental need to obey those rules that are the only guarantee of good, or at least improved, health.

It may be asked whether gorillas and other primates living in natural surroundings and eating what they instinctively choose have 'EEG abnormality'. There certainly seems to be no reason to suppose that any of them suffer from B12 deficiency. Dr E. Lester Smith and others have suggested that apes in the wild get their fair share simply because they pick it up from excreta and other such bonuses about which they are not over-fastidious. I am not qualified to argue in scientific terms with such distinguished authorities, but it is difficult to suppress the feeling that nature must have found a less haphazard way of ensuring that the apes get what they need. Primitive man, it follows, did not suffer from any undue obsession with hygiene, and therefore got along all right, but plenty of modern men are also none too fussy and it does not seem to have been established that B12 deficiency is confined to the nanny-trained and clinically pernickety members of the human community.

It is not a problem that can be solved by studying the EEG's and B12 levels in apes, because although it is known that some species of monkeys kept in captivity on a clean vegan diet can suffer from B12 deficiency, it is also known that it is not possible to draw accurate and relevant conclusions from the study of organisms removed from their natural habitat – a fact that forms one of the biggest scientific arguments against animal experiments. B12 deficiency in a captive monkey living on sterilised nuts is not proof that cleanliness has caused the deficiency. Not, that is, cleanliness per se. Stress – whether from wrong feeding, noise, fear, imprisonment, boredom, or any other result of upsetting an organism's normal pattern and rhythm of life – invalidates almost every conclusion drawn from study of creatures in captive and unnatural conditions.

Looking at the B12 question objectively, and in the light of what little is really known rather than conjectured, it does seem improbable in view of man's chemical and physiological similarity to the higher primates that vegans should fail to get enough B12 in a diet that befits their nearest known relatives; it seems more likely that if the puzzle has a chemical answer, it may be the freshness and instinctive choice of an ape's food that gives him what some vegans and omnivores lack. The fact that meat-eaters can also suffer from B12 deficiency makes it impossible to assert that actual lack of intake of B12 in human food is necessarily responsible, and I believe it is therefore more reasonable to give less attention to dietetic shortage of B12 than to the fundamental reasons for individual inability to benefit from the probably very small amount man needs for his proper functioning.

It seems, indeed, reasonable to pursue the possibility that the physical and nervous complications attributed to B12 deficiency have much more to do with the nature of our civilised lives than with the need for a vitamin in amounts in excess of what is sufficient for the other primates. This must, as implied, leave open-ended the question of whether the freshness and choice factors are crucial, but pending any more conclusive findings in this field it seems to me that we might do better to seek to understand B12 deficiency and many other ills in the light of, and in proportion to, our general departure from an environment and way of life that would be consistent with our physical structure.

If a diet free of all animal products is for most vegans perfectly adequate, then for such people it can presumably be rightly termed 'natural'. Possibly they have simply not been thrown into so unnatural a balance as have meat-eaters and those vegans who depend upon excessive(?) quantities of B12. It may be found that we should be working on the assumption not that we need so much B12, but that we *don't* need something else: as suggested, civilisation, or some nutrient or combination of modern refined foods that is acting against either the natural synthesising of B12 in the human body, or the truly healthy and uncontaminated organism's ability to function without B12. Dr Lester Smith's observation that although controversy persists as to the occurrence of B12 in higher plants, there is enough to be nutritionally significant in foodstuffs consumed in large quantities (Smith, E. Lester, *Vitamin B12*, Methuen 1965), suggests that herbivorous and frugivorous species should not need a higher intake of the vitamin than they will absorb from their normal diet.

In general, it should be noted, the health of vegans is good (Ellis F. R.; Montegriffo, V. M. E., op. cit.), as might be expected among people whose body weight is lighter than average, whose cholesterol and blood urea levels are lower, and whose consumption of more fibrous food than is usual among flesh-eaters almost certainly diminishes the likelihood of developing those various and often serious diseases to which the overloaded and frequently costive systems of many meat-eaters are all too prone.

This is not an attempt to argue against those scientists whose knowledge in this field is far greater than my own; but rather – accepting that scientists themselves are still far from agreement – to review some of the salient points and suggest a change of emphasis. None of the great men of science would deny that specialists often work from incorrect or insufficiently broad assumptions. In this instance, perhaps the questionable assumption concerns what may be fairly regarded as the norm. As the incidence of B12 deficiency symptoms in vegans is very small, and is also found in omnivores with seemingly adequate B12 intake, it is perhaps time that research into the problem became far more fundamental. I believe the answers may be found when there is a greater balance, a more profound recognition of those laws by which this planet's total ecology is governed, and to which mankind is no exception. Although it might well be wise for people who are changing from a meat-based diet to a vegan diet to take B12 supplements, as a way of reducing the possible shock to the system, this is not an admission or evidence that our species inherently needs to add to the B12 found naturally in plant life; rather, it suggests that having thrown our chemistry 'out of gear' we should be cautious in moving towards a more natural and sane way of life (imprisoned men have resisted their first taste of freedom and sunlight). That sanity, I am quite convinced, cannot be established while we maintain an exploitative, unscientific and profoundly selfish attitude to our total environment.

Notes

1. Half measures always produce problems of where to draw the line. The lacto-vegetarian whose concern is primarily with the cruelty aspect is in a particularly difficult position. Although the definition of a vegetarian that is accepted by the British and most other vegetarian societies is 'one who abstains from the use of flesh, fish and fowl, with or without the addition of eggs and dairy produce', the problem remains, for those who wish to face it, of deciding whether the greater cruelty lies in the eating of eggs and dairy products, or fish. Neither an egg nor a piece of cheese is in itself so obviously related to a sentient victim as is a dead herring complete from head to tail. A wild pigeon who leaves an egg on my cabbage patch will not find me spurning her offering on the grounds of conscience, though I'd prefer the cabbage. Is there most suffering involved in eating a kipper, an omelette or a fondu? How do we assess the element of suffering? Is the coldness of a fish's blood a clue to the degree of suffering involved in its death? On the other hand, what is it like to 'drown' in the air, and how many fish are gutted while still alive on board the factory ships? When one considers that a single hen will produce some hundreds of eggs in its lifetime, should one 'divide' the suffering in its life and death by the number of eggs it has produced, in order to arrive at the pain-content of a single egg? Equally, should one 'divide' the suffering of a cow and its calves by the pounds and gallons of butter, cheese and milk that the cow's life-span has produced? I know this begins to sound ridiculous to many people, but the lacto-vegetarian is not on firm ground in stopping short of veganism, and he could achieve greater consistency by examining and deciding upon such considerations individually. Some may calculate that despite the definition of vegetarianism that has been quoted, it may be the lesser of two evils to eat fish (or perhaps just some fish) than eggs or dairy produce. Only the vegan can afford to ignore the question.

2. To put the horse more squarely before the cart, there is a good deal of support for the theory that man lost his ability to manage without dietary B12 when he took to meat-eating, which caused the bacterium *Escherichia coli* to move further down his intestinal tract to beyond the point at which the B12 could be absorbed (see A. G. Long and F. Wokes, 'Vitamins and Minerals in Plants', *Plant Foods for Human Nutrition*, Vol. 1, No. 1, May 1968). The upward movement of the *Escherichia*, it may be, is encouraged by a return to that vegan pattern we abandoned. However, the inner reaches of our guts are not of universal fascination and most of us prefer to leave the problems of bacterial balance to the scientists. I must leave it to the really keen reader to explore for himself in greater depth.

Eight

Human or Humane?

That the predatory way of life is still observed by newer forms of life is in its measure an indictment against them. It is in principle a status quo persisted in after becoming due to disappear. 'Might is right' as a principle in the newest phase of life would seem doomed because it exemplifies in principle a status quo. Therefore, that predaceous man has an immensely long tradition behind him is no sanction for him; it may be an excuse, but it is no authorisation; it would authorise anachronism. It would seem that homo praedatorious is in a backwater unreached by the tide which set in some millennia since.

What is it then that poisons Nature? The cruelty of life ... In(man) evolving mind has got so far as to become critical of life. He feels the curse as well as the blessing attached to 'zest-to-live'. He is impressed by a cruelty inherent in the economy of life. He is disillusioned the more to find he is a part of that same dispensation. The régime is, if he asks his 'heart', one for which he cannot seek his heart's approval.

Sir Charles Sherrington, *Man on his Nature*

... the cruelty that goes on under the barbarous régime we call civilisation.

Thomas Hardy in a letter to Florence Henneker
on man's treatment of animals

The great discovery of the nineteenth century, that we are of one blood with the lower animals, has created new ethical obligations which have not yet penetrated the public conscience. The clerical profession has been lamentably remiss in preaching this obvious duty.

Dean Inge

> *They sniffed, poor things, for their green fields,*
> *They cried so loud I could not sleep;*
> *For fifty thousand shillings down*
> *I would not sail again with sheep.*

W. H. Davies

The unpardonable forgetfulness in which the lower animals have hitherto been left by the moralists of Europe is well known. It is pretended that the beasts have no rights. They persuade themselves that our conduct in regard to them has nothing to do with morals or (to speak the language of their morality) that we have no duties towards animals; a doctrine revolting, gross and barbarous ...

Schopenhauer

Before the first word of this book was written, the last chapter was planned to consist of precise details of some of the many cruelties our species inflicts on those eatable creatures we sacrifice daily and in vast numbers to our uncaring greed and cowardice. Volumes could be produced to support the moral, compassionate and aesthetic reasons for moving from an animal economy to one based on plant life. Endless stomach-turning, mind-sickening, even heart-touching examples could be quoted of the torments that are inflicted upon fear-knowing, pain-feeling living beings – torments that we know only too well go on, but of which we do not wish to receive uncomfortable reminders.

Yet it would not be an original exercise to list mankind's brutalities. Many have done so and their works for the most part have been respectfully received or silently ignored, and then forgotten. To quote cruelty as a basis for reform may be pardonable; it seldom gets attention.

So it is more realistic, perhaps, not to concentrate for too long on the barbarities that anyone who thinks knows perfectly well are going on incessantly. It would be easy enough to paint in all too accurately strong colours a picture of, for instance, calves born without the will to live or even to suck ('liveability' is an example of current farming newspeak) – many of them lucky (if that is the word) if they are allowed more than two or three days to live at all; to convey some measure of the physical agony experienced by the two million whales, dolphins and porpoises slaughtered in the past fifty years with such brutality, for products obtainable from plant and mineral sources; to invite pity for the prolapsed hen dragging her guts around (if permitted the freedom to walk) until she dies of weakness or cannibalism; to stress that (to take only a single statistic) over 300 million battery hens come off the conveyor belt every year in Great Britain alone; to point to the fact that pigs can literally die of fright prior to slaughter – a danger so well known to farmers that they will feed them linseed meal or vitamin E medicines, lack of vitamin E being associated with myocardial infarction (heart attack); to add that thousands of millions of this, that or the other specially bred animal or bird are slaughtered yearly so that a proportion of the human species can continue to eat what it wants – but does not need – to eat; to condemn the vested interests that have latched on to the farmers' rapacity, offering a range of powerful drugs not under the supervision of a vet or a doctor and marketed solely by the persuasion of merchants, regardless of their suitability and side-effects; to suggest that we hide our slaughter-houses and other centres of animal suffering behind high walls and in out-of-the-way places precisely because we know only too well what is necessary if we are to indulge our greed; to emphasise that in pressing for the abolition or moderation of 'factory-farming' methods – as do organisations that have done such sincerely motivated good work as has Compassion in World Farming – we are in danger of deceiving ourselves that controlled, reduced or alternative cruelty is adequate concession to humane conscience; to argue at length that not only have other creatures a right to live but (and more to the point within a system that breeds domesticated species solely for consumption of their flesh and by-products) they have the even more critical right not to be born at all at the whim of man; to prove, in short, that in our half-baked thinking and incessant ferocity towards the countless sentient creatures whom, alive, we imprison, mutilate, maim, trap, strangle, shoot, hook, chase, snare, de-limb, behead, suffocate, flay, disembowel, stab, crush, over-feed, burn, drown, boil, freeze, cut up, make sick, terrorise and by numerous other means mercilessly exploit day in and day out for no better reason than that we wish to devour them, we are shamefully forsaking that one obligation which above all others we should recognise – to put our unique knowledge of the difference between good and evil, between mercy and cruelty, before our heart-hardening greed.

It is relevant and interesting to compare the articles on slaughtering that have appeared in the *Encyclopaedia Britannica* over the past 100 years. In the 9th edition (1875), under 'Abattoir', can be found two pages of explicit description, showing a taking-it-for-granted insensitivity towards the least savoury of trades. In each edition since, the matter is given less prominence, both in graphic detail and in length. The most recent edition has almost phased out the subject altogether, relegating it to a sub-heading under 'meat and Meat-packing'. It is significant, perhaps, that so prominent a growth industry should receive such declining attention. Is it more realistic to attribute this to a growing sense of shame than to an increase in callous indifference? The question must be left open.

It would seem as pointless to go into greater details of our abominable behaviour towards the other creatures with whom we share this planet as it would be to elaborate on the statistics of *human* suffering and misery – with the figures for cruelty to children, for instance, which are of no less concern to those who have faced up to the totality of men's savagery. For it is not just the known numbers of babies and young boys and girls who are physically and visibly assaulted by brutalised adults that are so appalling, but also the incalculable number of cases where all that greed and selfishness is directed in innumerable less overt ways against young creatures towards whom we should be most expected to direct our love and concern.

Easy as it would be to draw the parallel at considerable length, what good would be done? Those who already know what we do, either care or don't care. No amount of proof or persuasion concerning the mere rights and sufferings of other living beings will alter the majority of human's behaviour a jot. Schooled early enough in insensitivity, there are all too many

117

of our kind who can spend a lifetime without experiencing a twinge of pity, although afforded every opportunity to open their minds and hearts to the facts of mankind's pitiless treatment of its own and other species.

This is why it has seemed best to place most emphasis on two other important aspects of the vegetarian argument in this book, showing why we all stand to benefit from a more humane diet in, firstly, the short term (through adopting a diet for which we are chemically and physiologically better attuned) and, secondly, the long term (because of the ecological and economic facts of modern life that we can no longer afford to ignore). For most of us these are more powerful arguments than anything so irrelevant to our daily lives as mere unkindness to animals. The poverty of the human imagination, the strength of greed, the shortness of memory, the pressures to which we are subjected in business and family life, and our willingness to believe only what we want to believe – these are the barriers that have confronted anyone who has ever taken a clear look at the natural world and has been anguished by the rapacious and pitiless part played by the human race.

Inasmuch as any of us are concerned at all by such matters, most of us are satisfied by what Curtis Freshel called The Legislative Illusion – those measures taken to modify or make acceptable some of our cruelties, rather than to renounce them. It has been said, of course, that if we cared about suffering and injustice; about the facts of politics, poverty and war; about starving nations; about the true extent of child, adult and animal misery that lies below that unsubmerged one millionth of the iceberg that sticks above the sea of newsprint from which most of us make our judgements of the condition of the world we live in – if we really cared about and concentrated on these things 'we should go mad, no doubt, and die that way'. Possibly, in their wisdom, the mind-controllers know, or think they know, that there must be a limit to what we can take.

Yet even as one writes these words one knows that the idea is a nonsense. It is just one more thing that it is comfortable to believe. Like the man who sought treatment for his inferiority complex only to be told by the psychiatrist 'But, Mr Jones, you *are* inferior,' most of us are quite incapable, in our present state of mis-education and self-obsession, of seeing even ourselves for what we are – far less the world that surrounds us. Most of us can take in little more than our daily problems of personal survival – because that is all we are trained to do. And even these we get wrong, believing (and conveying to our children the belief) that what matters above all is the kind of money we are bringing home, the sort of materially successful image we are showing to our neighbours, and the degree of credit our children can bring to us.

These are harsh words. I would be sorry if they antagonised the very people whose imaginations and better feelings I most wish to see expand. But the process of living has taught me that the very most one can hope for is to make a few facts and ideas available to that small but never insignificant minority that is concerned with the fundamentals of human life and values. That minority will have realised that such fundamentals can be imparted only through a more mature concept of education, and they will be convinced that despite apparently overwhelming evidence to the contrary there can be found within the human heart and mind some spark that, when activated and cherished, will eventually prove that the rôle of man has not all along been that of the devil's advocate, but rather that of a species destined – self-destined, if you distrust the 'grand-design' concept – to create order out of chaos, reason out of nonsense, purpose out of futile misdirection, and the quality of mercy and pity out of a background of almost unrelieved savagery.

But what have we made of education to date? We worship academic distinction – mere aptitude for absorbing facts and passing examinations. It seems we have yet to learn that it is not the power to absorb facts that makes us properly educated and superior to the other apes, but the power of imagination. The difference between a chimpanzee and an academic can be, in both senses of the phrase, no more than a matter of degree. Only insofar as our imaginations guide and enrich that sponge-like organ we are too often inclined to confuse with a truly developed mind, have we any cause to hope for better things for the world and for ourselves.

If there is any justification whatsoever for our species to be around at all, its function has to be something on the lines indicated in the penultimate paragraph. If we do not believe this to be so, then we must believe in something far worse than any jungle could ever have thought up. We do not need to confuse the issue with religious slogans or sociological jargon in order to see that if mankind continues on its present path of environmental and self destruction it will have achieved far less of real worth than the earthworm or a vulture. If all we can do in the world is to make it bloodier and beastlier and more artificial than it was when our race took the first wrong turning, we would be doing ourselves and our environment a great kindness in bringing the whole episode to a rapid close. A species that has gone so far wrong as has our own is not going to stand still. It must either improve or get worse. I do not believe that the latter choice is necessary any more than it is desirable. I have to believe that the former is possible, and if I did not I would not have bothered to write this book.

The authors of such books as *The Limits to Growth, The Greening of America, Small is Beautiful, To Be or Not to Be*, and many another, would probably say much the same. Whether one speaks in dry terms about 'global equilibrium' or, more emotively, about human cruelty and those 'behaviour patterns' that at one time we numbered up to seven and rightly termed 'deadly', the basic concern is to some extent shared. We are all deeply disturbed by the way the world is going. It has been my own brief to attempt to concentrate on a single – but I believe immensely important – aspect of mankind's failure to contribute to his environment something he is perfectly capable of contributing if only he can be tempted to see the reasons for so doing.

Cruelty is the worst sin of all. It might almost be called the only one. A form of obsession with self and excluding consideration of others, cruelty has to go before any other reform of ourselves or our environment begins to be possible. The cruelty inherent in our exploitation of the animal world is so undoubted that anyone who has read this far and now finds himself in disagreement with such a statement will have wasted his time, for he will be so far from knowing what I am talking about that he will never have suffered a moment's pang about anything at all that is going on in the world outside his own immediate circle. I believe and hope that there are few intelligent people who have declined to such a low of ignorance and self-obsession, though we have to face that very many of us have allowed the scum of daily pollution so to cloud our consciences that the truth and importance of what really matters – of what it is really all about – have been lost to sight.

There are, as we all know, no reasons for indulging in cruelty. The arguments for a humane treatment of other creatures cannot be refuted except by a nihilist. Such arguments are answered not by reasons, but by excuses. When such excuses are accompanied by deference to the theory rather than the practice of idealism, the result is that most human of human failings, hypocrisy. Excuses provide the easy way out, the path of least effort and continued self-indulgence. The educated and intelligent person who pays lip service to morality, and has at least intelligently faced the inexcusable nature of flesh-eating, is more difficult to excuse than the unthinking, who have thought about little, and see no alternative. Most of us prefer to fall back on the childish defence of 'But I want to' rather than accept the necessity for self-reform. Dispensing our compassion with absurd selectivity – shedding crocodile tears over the bull-fight or the mauled bird brought in by the cat, while in the next breath crooning over the tenderised flesh of the castrated steer or the caponised fowl – few of us have progressed further than the picturebook clichés of our child-hood. We want the grass to be green, the sky to be blue, and no splashes of red except on the poppies and the instantly recognised 'baddies'.

It may be possible to understand and to feel some pity for the weakness and gullibility of our species, but when we look at what our failings have made of the world, and the hell that we have created for its more defenceless inhabitants, it is surely incumbent on everyone who can see the total picture to put that understanding at the disposal of those weaker creatures who need it most.

Before it is too late we must become aware that this earth we live on is not anthropocentric. Only man is man-centred. Ecologically speaking, we are totally dispensable. The biosphere is in no way dependent on man and would in fact be much better off without him. The environmentalists who have suggested that man is like a fatal disease that the earth has been unfortunate enough to contract are not indulging in absurd exaggeration. We have the power of choice. We can help what we do. Animals cannot. It is up to us to realise the necessity to ourselves and to our environment to become an influence for good rather than for evil – to learn to live symbiotically instead of like parasites and rogue predators who kill without need or even hatred. The fox, some may protest, kills in excess of need, and therefore animals are no better than man. But if man chooses to upset the local ecology by his own predatoriness, and then creates an artificial situation in which a quantity of poultry is held captive in a small area, he cannot complain when a fox starts to behave like a man. We cannot justify our own actions by citing those of a fox or any other animal when man behaves far worse by breeding and slaughtering thousands of pheasants, grouse, cattle, sheep, pigs and other victims of his 'sport' and stomach.

In a way this all boils down to the only viable kind of morality being little more than a sense of balance. In my last book I suggested that only by a change of values, not by a change of political administrators from the same stable as their predecessors, can people learn to behave more like *humane* beings. Unregenerate people can only create an unregenerate organisation and an unregenerate society. Only better people can create a better society. They do not even have to create it – it is already there by the very act of self-improvement. By 'better people' I was meaning, above all, more compassionate people: people who have seen the paramount necessity to eradicate their cruelties. For cruelty is humanity's worst form of imbalance.

There is no parallel in nature to mankind's cruelty. It is a unique vice, peculiar to man, and the cause of the major ills of our society. Oddly enough, despite the state of the world by which so many of us are now downright scared, there are still plenty of people around who breathe brimstone at the very suggestion that people should become better. They get, it seems, an instant vision of mere goody-goodiness, or interfering busy-bodying, and probably a reduction of their sex life. Let them be assured that although all sorts of baddy-baddiness may well get tidied up in the course of our educating ourselves into a more balanced concept of life and our responsibilities, it is above all cruelty in its many forms that is the evil we must concentrate on eradicating. There is no more constant and widespread example of this evil than in our daily treatment of other species.

The eradication of cruelty is an educational problem, little more. But two great hurdles stand in the way. The first of these is man's fierce resistance to change – personal change, that is, of habits and heart. We all know only too well that one of the major irritants within a consumer society is change for the sake of change, but this relates only to such idiocies as planned obsolescence and other short cuts to high profits and low standards. The kind of change that can come about through increasing knowledge leading to a revision of habits established in times of greater ignorance is a rarer but much more important phenomenon.

But it is coming. Current awareness of this necessity to examine old patterns has been exemplified by the views of the executive committee of the Club of Rome in their commentary on the findings published in *The Limits to Growth*, a report for the Club of Rome's project on the predicament of mankind. In each of the points made is to be found an unequivocal concern with the basic problem that has to be resolved – man's preparedness to alter his thought patterns and life-styles:

> ... new forms of thinking that will lead to a fundamental revision of human behaviour and, by implication, of the entire fabric of present-day society; ... an overall strategy must be evolved to attack all major problems, including in particular those of man's relationship with his environment; ... we cannot expect technological solutions alone to get us out of this vicious circle; ... to define the balances that must exist within human society, and between human society and its habitat, and to perceive the consequences that may ensue when such balances are disrupted; ... we affirm finally that any deliberate attempt to reach a rational and enduring state of equilibrium by planned measures, rather than by chance or catastrophe, must ultimately be founded on a basic change of values and goals at individual, national and world levels; ... only the conviction that there is no other avenue to survival can liberate the moral, intellectual and creative forces required to initiate this unprecedented human undertaking; ... the last thought we wish to offer is that man must explore himself – his goals and values – as much as the world he seeks to change. The dedication to both tasks must be unending. The crux of the matter is not only whether the human species will survive, but even more whether it can survive without falling into a state of worthless existence.

Excellent though it is to see such phrases peppering a dry, factual report by environmentalists, scientists, educators, humanists, industrialists and civil servants, it has to be pointed out that they are saying no more than has been said again and again over the centuries. The trouble has been that the urgency – the threats to mankind itself – have not been sufficiently apparent for the vast majority of people, or even a significant minority, to take a blind bit of notice.

It does not follow that man's new awareness of his responsibilities to his environment has yet shown many signs of recognising his moral obligations towards other sentient life forms. But it has begun to dawn on him that as a consequence of his more mature concern for the human race and its total environment, a new attitude towards the so-called lesser creatures is inescapable. If this is not the same thing as a conscious compassion or even a guilty conscience, it is at least a step in the right direction.

If willing to start thinking on these lines, one must to some extent be influenced by evidence that many of the greatest names of past and present have not merely anticipated the corporate wisdom shown in the Club of Rome's report, but have made clear that the logical extension of that kind of reasoning must result in, or at least demand, a more responsible and humane concern for the animal kingdom. No 'basic change of values and goals at individual, national and world levels' can prevent man 'falling into a state of worthless existence' unless he is prepared to tackle that violence and cruelty into which he has been schooled throughout the sanguinary history of his species.

And 'schooled' is the right word. It is, I believe, a nonsense – a sophisticated distortion whose perpetuation in all too many spheres has created the second great hurdle to a better concept of education – to suggest that man is innately violent and aggressive. Fear and anger will produce 'aggression' in very many species; but 'aggression' is simply not the right word for that channelling of physical energy that is stimulated by dangerous and provoking circumstances that have nothing to do with a cold and calculated determination to harm or plunder. The bulk of men's cruelty is the result of the barbarous goals and values they have been educated to accept as right and normal. To this very day a high proportion of all taught history focuses interminably upon tediously similar and uninstructive examples of warring, rapacious man's planned abominations against his own kind.

The young are seeing this increasingly and, for all that some of them have taken part in herd demonstrations that have provoked degrees of physical violence, they are reacting against those institutions and vested interests which seek to maintain the exploitational *status quo*. Because they have been taught nothing else, they can hardly be blamed for the fact that much of their reaction has so far been little better than the system to which they are opposed, but their responses to the pressures of militarism, industrialisation and the whole web of competitive materialism that shrouds the highly developed areas of the world are – unless an expression of mere political brainwashing – a heartening indication that an instinctual reasonableness still exists.

When we discuss unorthodox matters we tend to forget that while dissenters who voice their arguments stick out like sore thumbs, the majority are silent – not because they have thought whether their habits are responsible, wise or necessary, but because they just have not thought. Very few eminent men or women with a balanced and civilised concern, who have considered the question of mankind's responsibility towards other species, have seriously suggested that it is necessary or even defensible to breed, slaughter and consume the animal kingdom.

On the contrary, while most of them may not have felt the need, or found the opportunity, to make any public or published pronouncements on such matters, it is probably true to say that the majority of those who have considered the matter at all have quite categorically come down on the side of the animals. This is not to say that all those who have championed the non-human species have necessarily gone so far as to refrain from eating them. 'A meat diet is far from satisfying,' said Livingstone, but lacking evidence to the contrary one suspects he went on being unsatisfied, if for no better reason than that he was so inordinately busy exploring the Zambezi and worrying about the sources of the Nile. We all tend to spend a large part of our time 'worrying about the sources of the Nile', so that rich or poor, famous or failure, we unthinkingly slide into many habits that a moment's quiet consideration would show us to be absurd, inconsistent, or even downright anti-social and self-destructive.

It is because it is impossible to over-emphasise the importance of the rôle education plays in the civilising process that this book contains the comments of a number of distinguished men and women whose words would have been so much more profitably heeded than the blood-spattered pages of those past-distorting history books and translations of the ancient classics that have done so much to cement the impression that the facts of life have been little more than those of destruction and death. It is the realisations of such men and women that must be allowed to inform that 'reschooling' that Duncan Williams has argued so forcefully is essential if the techniques of survival – dependent upon so much more than mere technology – are to be properly learned. Our academic centres, at all levels, are in urgent need of a reasoned compassion. As Williams has written (*To Be or Not to Be*, Davis-Poynter Ltd, London, 1974):

> Reason alone can be hard, unimaginative and selfish; unalloyed passion and emotionalism can be sentimental, cloying and egotistical. The fusion of the two was the *beau idéal* of the best minds of the early eighteenth century, with sentimentality (as opposed to sentiment) waiting in the wings, to emerge from 1750 onwards as the dominant mood both in literary and social terms.

Of the numerous recent writers who have seen the necessity to relate this fusion to the treatment of those many species we are big enough and brainy enough to dominate and outwit, John Galsworthy is today one of those least associated with such realisations. Yet he saw very clearly that all sentient life is an inseparable part of an inter-related pattern. His vision was essentially that of the enlightened environmentalist of today:

> You are not living in a private world all of your own. Everything you say and do and think has its effect on everybody around you. For example, if you feel and say loudly enough that it is an infernal shame to keep larks and other wild song-birds in cages, you will infallibly infect a number of other people with that sentiment, and in course of time those people who feel as you do will become so numerous that larks, thrushes, blackbirds and linnets will no longer be caught and kept in cages. ... When a thing exists which you really abhor, I wish you would remember a little whether in letting it strictly alone you are minding your own business on principle, or simply because it is comfortable to do so.

Minding your own business because it is more comfortable to do so is repeatedly cited as a besetting sin of modern man; a part of that cowardice that hardens us against personal change. Enormous indignation, often fully justified, is shown by journalists concerned with human poverty, homelessness and neglect; with baby-battering; with landscape destruction, urban ugliness, architectural insensitivity and litter-loutishness; with the problems of old age in a world that cares too little; with the problems of youth in a world that cares too much about exploiting and mis-educating the young. On these and many other issues the socially-conscious media man does much to arouse the feelings of his readers. And good luck to him where his concern is genuine and his facts correct. But although his strictures have embraced a certain amount of disquiet about factory-farming, the export and transport of live animals prior to slaughter, and the barbarities of seal-hunting and whaling, it is only once in a blue moon that the mass-circulation media permit a genuine and full examination of whether the basic uses to which animals are put, and because of which innumerable cruelties are inevitable, can be justified. Perhaps it is feared that if you make your reader or viewer feel really uncomfortable, you may lose him.

It is far safer to fool oneself and others that with a little bit of tightening up here, and a little more supervision there, everything that we wish to do with animals, and damned well intend to go on doing with them, will soon be within 'permissible' limits of suffering.

We no longer have any excuse for such cowardice and hypocrisy. We are fed with too much information to be able to pretend any longer that we do not know what is done to living, feeling creatures in order that we may cling to the interminable meat-and-two-veg routine that with minor variations is still the centrepiece of Western culinary art.

Some may protest: 'Oh, but things have improved so much lately.

125

People are more concerned. Cruelty and suffering have been reduced to a minimum.' Many of them genuinely gulled by The Legislative Illusion, they point to some Bill passed, usually after repeated readings and blockings in Parliament, to ameliorate some one aspect of our fundamentally unchanged insensitivity towards the creatures we wish to eat, chase, torture or wear; and because public concern is still so feeble, such Bills are little more than a sop to minority feeling, their implementation being in the hands of breeders, slaughterers, inspectors and government officials who know all too well the shortness of public memory and the power of commercial interests to over-ride almost any measure that is backed not by the pursuit of profit and power, but by mere abstract whimsy-whamsiness about kindness to animals.

These may seem harsh comments, perhaps. But the facts about what we do to animals are harsh. Whatever affection individuals may feel for domestic pets, collectively human beings do not allow, and in many cases doubtless feel they cannot afford to allow, pity to influence the decisions that they make in their jobs and social lives. Although it is true that people know more today (or at least have no excuse for not knowing), their concern has made only short inroads on their behaviour. They are still far more concerned with what other people think about them than with doing what the briefest reflection would tell them is more humane.

But even supposing I have got the balance of despair and hope about right, we do not dispose of the problem by saying 'Yes, how true!' and then ignoring the consequences. We have got to take ourselves in hand, and in order to do this we must face the implication of certain facts. If we can accept that one of these is that modern, Western education has gone tragically wrong in its choice of methods and targets, we shall be thinking on the right lines, but I cannot over-emphasise that until the violence and cruelty that is enshrined in the educative influence of modern society (by which I mean in the junior schools and the home even more than in the later academic environment) is replaced by something more civilised, the fate of all sentient life – our own, not just the so-called 'lesser creatures' – can only be sad and sanguinary. We get out of life only what we put into it, for all that this often means that the innocent suffer while the guilty get away with murder.

When we look at what the over-inquisitive, monkey mind of the Aberrant Ape has made of the world, leading us into so many unnatural habits and changing so many aspects of the natural world itself into parodies of what should be, it is not difficult to see why religious and philosophical systems have come about. There are times when many of us must wonder if we are not going mad trying to find explanations for why our species behaves so insanely. Things that are obvious to people who keep their

126

eyes and minds open and receptive are, seemingly, not seen or understood at all by those who 'only think they think'. Our attitude to animal life is very much a case in point. Because they wish to exploit and torment 'inferior' beings, the mass of humans have long persuaded themselves that only their own species can experience real feeling or thought.

Although many pay lip-service to a crude yardstick of suffering based arbitrarily on size or 'cuddle-worthiness' (few hesitate to crush an ant, but feel some pity for a sick or wounded elephant; the koala bear attracts more sentiment than the skunk), most of us will fall over backwards to avoid anything that smacks of that dirty word anthropomorphism. 'Oh, yes, there may be some rudimentary feeling of discomfort,' say these sages comfortably on hearing the suggestion that a grouse dying of its maggot-infested wounds under a bush, or a stuck pig losing its screams in a gargle of blood, might be experiencing an unpleasant departure, 'but there is no thought there; no anticipation.'

It would be fruitless to argue to what extent each species of animal, bird or fish can feel, think, anticipate, or suffer mental or physical pain, but it takes an extraordinarily well-developed state of self-deception to ignore the evidence for animals' ability to experience excruciating levels of physical pain, and even to feel sorrow of a kind and to a degree that is pathetically 'human'.

Higher animals most certainly do think, though their thoughts may be smaller. We do not need laboratory conditions to tell us this. As anyone who has kept a dog knows full well, they reason – if only for short distances. The actions of dogs, cats, horses, monkeys and many other creatures – perhaps, for all we know, even down to the levels of insect life – are quite obviously prompted by reason. Pavlov's experiments told us only what most of us preferred to believe, not what all of us should know.

In some respects animals are streets ahead of us mentally. A dog will telepathically know the thought of a walk in its master's mind even before the coat or boots are put on or a move has been made from the armchair. If, as is well known, animals have this telephathic faculty so much better developed than have human beings, to what extent are our crimes against them even greater than most of us are prepared to admit? If there is doubt in any answer to this question, as there must be, that doubt should alone be enough to make us stay our hands against all other sentient life.

If we think about it – and not many of us do – there are two main night-mares in our world – what men do to each other and what they do to other species. The connection between the two has as yet gone almost un-recognised. Yet this is, or should be, what ecological morality is all about. For one does not need to be a seer, a scientist, a sectarian or even a sociologist (who ought to be a compound of all three, but seldom is) to work out the simple but generally ignored fact that the total world situation is not going to be improved if evolution's leading animal imagines that its only moral obligation is towards its own kind. Bible or no bible, cruelty begets cruelty, violence breeds violence, and the exploitation and greed of which man is so uniquely capable cannot simply be switched off like a light when he turns from his rape of the animal world to the difficult problems of social relationships within his own species.

As Professor Bruce Allsopp has written, 'Ecological morality requires of the individual that he be the best he can be so that the sum of individual contributions to the communality should be a sum of excellencies' (*Ecological Morality*, Muller, 1972). Allsopp shows a leaning towards the necessity for an eclectic outlook in a world dominated by mind-narrowing specialisms and compartmentalism when he adds: 'We must not seek to achieve perfection along one road, but should, on the contrary, endeavour to create the conditions in which human life may be enriched by innumerable different contributions.'

Human life cannot be enriched in any ultimate or even short-term sense if it pays no regard to our obligations to the rest of 'creation'. It just is not enough to take the easy-going, so-called liberal view of the homely, 'human' kind of man who for reasons that on analysis are probably totally selfish is against the early (i.e., in his lifetime) alteration of the status quo. Our crying need is for the universal and early adoption of at least a basic framework of moral conviction, within which our attitude to animals cannot fail to have a considerable place. Without this framework we are wallowing around in the truly 'permissive' world of non-commitment. 'Oh, tolerance,' someone might well have written, 'what crimes have been committed in your name?' Non-violence, or the nearest we can get to it, is one basic the world has got to accept if it is to survive. The necessity to curb our unrestricted human spawning is another. The infestation of a species is in itself a form of violence to the environment. An ecological immorality.

I hope and believe that a few readers at least may have been helped by this book to accept that our species must establish and maintain a beneficial relationship with the rest of nature. It cannot be called beneficial unless it can be seen to extend and evolve permanently into the future. It must be a creative relationship, not a predatory one. Conservation is not enough. What this will mean – in our behaviour, in our sense of responsibility towards each other and the rest of the world – must be spelt out for each one of us from our earliest age, and this is what education is (or should be) all about.

'Yes, but you have spoiled your case by getting too emotional about it,' some may object, as though emotion was one of the major criminal tendencies rather than something – in its right place and properly informed – of which the world is in great need. But have I? The bulk of this book deals in hard, often brutal facts, amply supported by science, statistics and common knowledge. Where emotional appeals are based solidly on such facts, no case is thereby spoiled. It merely becomes painfully unacceptable to those who do not wish to accept it. As Brigid Brophy, who writes so brilliantly about our treatment of animals, has said, those who dare to emotionalise about animals are apt to be attacked instantly as sentimentalists, cranks, kill joys, people with no grasp on economic realities, twee anthropomorphisers who attribute human feelings (if not human names and clothes as well) to animals, actually preferring them to humans and readier to succour a stray cat than an orphan child. But such naïveté and shallowness of reaction is surely passing. The wider picture of which our attitude to the animals is an essential part is being studied with increasing concern. The test of a viewpoint, as Brophy has said, 'is its rationality, not the number of people who endorse it'.

It was Thomas Hardy who wrote: 'The establishment of the common origin of all species logically involves a readjustment of altruistic morals, by enlarging the application of what has been called the Golden Rule from the area of mere mankind to that of the whole animal kingdom.' It may have been Leslie Stephens' essay on Darwinism that prompted Hardy's remark, yet it was only one more restatement of a realisation that had been expressed over and over again long before the origin of the species was of interest to anyone. Unless one subscribes to the primitive and shocking belief that animals, being without souls, are fair game for whatever treatment humans wish to inflict on them, the obligation to show pity towards all sentient life is universally recognised as religious in the widest and best sense of that all too often narrow word. There are few religious beliefs that fail to emphasise the need for compassion. Unfortunately there are few scientific specialisms who grant it the least attention. While no theist who conceives of his god as aligned to the smallest degree of mercy can logically dismiss the right of all sentient beings to expect from man more than from the other members of creation evidence of the divine values of pity and love, the scientific mind has as yet shown little sign of awakening to this realisation. Yet without it mere knowledge is nothing more than contaminated dust.

Victor Hugo's *grande morale*, clearly sensed by Hardy and the many others whose concerns were religiously based, must be equally valid to the observant scientist and ecologist of the present day; and also to the young, many of whom have benefited from widening communications, have seen more of others' life-styles, have been appalled by the Establishment's destruction of any but the most mundane idealism, and are today searching

129

almost desperately for a philosophy by which to live in a world of increasing superficiality, violence and materialism.

Here, in the wide field of our treatment of other living beings, religion and science are capable of finding a unity on the very highest level of their separate specialisms. Here the balance born of humane eclecticism can bring about a vital and applicable ethic. There is, as was stressed in the first chapter, a moral order within the newly discovered science of ecology. This book has tried to show why a humane diet is, or can be, ecological man's number-one priority. It is becoming daily more obvious that the changeover (we might even say changeback) is to a large extent inevitable, especially if our numbers do not quickly decline. But it is vitally important, if there is a shred of reason for believing that mankind is working out some evolutionary pattern and accepting an obligation or profound need to grow spiritually, that we do the right things for the right reasons rather than for expediency or lack of alternative. I choose to end the main section of this book on a no more flourishing phrase than that, for it is as important as it is sober. I ask you to consider it.

Nine

As Old as Man

By confining his morality to his own species, man has become the most immoral of all animals; and in so far as the Earth is the Great Mother, and he himself one of her children, man is a matricide. His urgent need, for his own salvation, is a conviction of this sin.

We have failed to understand ourselves and our place in nature because we have been blinded by conceit. Our virtues are real, but they are not exclusive to ourselves. In societies far older than our own, the natural activities of mating, care of the young, and group-defence had already led to an expansion of the sense of self to include others, so that the female would give her life for her young and the male would give his life for the group ... When our dogs show these qualities habitually, we call them instinctive; when we ourselves display them now and then, we call them divine. And this is absolutely typical of the instinctive arrogance of man. ... man is a far more dangerous and unpredictable animal than was the extinct tyrannosaur, and may devastate the Earth by knowledge without love. The study of life without sympathy with it leads at best to a husk of learning and at worst to disastrous results. If we are to be creators and not destroyers, we need knowledge with love, taking from the one a new world-picture and from the other a new ethic.

John Vyvyan: *Sketch for a World -Picture*
(A Study of Evolution)

I, for my part, wonder of what sort of feeling, mind or reason that man was possessed who was first to pollute his mouth with gore, and allow his lips to touch the flesh of a murdered being; who spread his table with the mangled form of dead bodies, and claimed as daily food and dainty dishes what but now were beings endowed with movement, with perception and with voice.

Plutarch

Why should you call me to account for eating decently? If I battened on the scorched corpses of animals, you might well ask me why I did that.

George Bernard Shaw

Nothing more strongly arouses our disgust than cannibalism, yet we make the same impression on Buddhists and vegetarians, for we feed on babies, though not on our own.

Robert Louis Stevenson

131

We might as well eat the flesh of men as the flesh of other animals.

Diogenes

*I have no doubt that it is part of the destiny of the human race . . . to
leave off eating animals.*

Thoreau

IN the eight preceding chapters I have tried to present at least the out-
lines of the case for meat-eating mankind's return to a plant-based diet.
The main emphasis has been on the ecological, economic, health and nutritional aspects because these are possibly of most interest to those for
whom such ideas are relatively new.

There is, however, a large number of people for whom the history of
vegetarianism, and the literature of its ethical justification, are of equal
importance – if for no other reason than that it is comforting to know that
so far from being alone in one's concern at the inhumanity of man towards
other species, a very large number of past and present men and women have
condemned the cruelties we are prepared to inflict in order to gratify our
acquired taste for flesh and blood. Among older books little known to the
general public must be mentioned Porphyry's *On Abstinence from Animal
Food*, Humphrey Primatt's *A Dissertation on the Duty of Mercy and Sin of
Cruelty to Brute Animals*, and Shelley's *An Essay on the Vegetable System
of Diet* (possibly inspired by his friendship with John Newton whose work
The Return to Nature, published in 1811, is thought by some to mark the
beginning of the present era of vegetarianism).

Since Shelley's day little of substance was published until Howard
Williams' classic work *The Ethics of Diet*, and some excellent and equally
unobtainable books by the late Henry S. Salt, and the following pages
may go a short way to meeting the need for a modern summary of the
literature and development of this concern.

THE INFLUENCE OF RELIGION

Few thinking people today would deny that the failure of the church to
perpetuate a living faith has been due largely to its abandonment of
Christianity for Churchianity, and many young people in particular would
see the main charge against orthodox religious teaching as being that
theology, dogma and ritual have supplanted and obscured the simple
moral and spiritual directives of Jesus Christ.

This is very relevant to our theme. The churches' most blatant mis-
representation of Jesus's directives has been in the sphere of violence. As
Henry Salt wrote in his powerful book *Seventy Years Among Savages:*

Religion has never befriended the cause of humaneness. Its monstrous doctrine of
eternal punishment and the torture of the damned underlies much of the barbarity

132

with which man has treated man; and the deep division imagined by the Church between the human being, with his immortal soul, and with the soulless 'beasts', has been responsible for an incalculable sum of cruelty.

However, this is not the place to argue the matter in depth; but even the Bible (and one says 'even' for the simple reason that by selecting one's texts from that source one can find approval for practically every good or bad thing under the sun) starts off with God assuring mankind that He has 'given you every herb bearing seed, which is upon the face of all the earth, and every tree, in which is the fruit of a tree yielding seed; to you it shall be for meat' (Genesis i, 39). And later, with even more emphasis: 'But flesh with the life thereof, which is the blood thereof, shall ye not eat' (Genesis ix, 4).

In that direct translation of early Aramaic texts, *The Essene Gospel of Peace*, Jesus himself minced no words: 'And the flesh of slain beasts in his body will become his own tomb. For I tell you truly, he who kills, kills himself, and whoso eats the flesh of slain beasts, eats the body of death.'

In his book *The Gospel of the Holy Twelve*, the late G. J. Ouseley offers a translation of the original Gospel which members of the Essene community preserved from the general corruption. Here is a version of Jesus's teachings that has not been tampered with by the 'correctors' appointed by the ecclesiastical authorities of Nicea. These 'editors' cut out with minute care the teachings they were disinclined to emphasise or follow, in particular everything that might serve as an argument against flesh-eating, such as the account of Jesus's interference on several occasions to save animals from ill treatment, and even that interesting and important teaching – ever prominent in eastern scriptures – of the essential unity of all life.

The community in which Joseph and Mary lived did not slaughter a lamb to celebrate the Feast of the Passover. 'Now Joseph and Mary, his parents, went up to Jerusalem every year at the Feast of the Passover, and observed the feast after the manner of their brethren, who abstained from bloodshed and the eating of flesh and from strong drink.'

The Essene text indicates that from childhood Jesus was loving and protective towards animals and birds. 'And to all he spake, saying: "Keep yourselves from blood and things strangled, and from dead bodies of birds and beasts, and from all deeds of cruelty and from all that is gotten of wrong. Think ye that the blood of beasts and of birds will wash away sin?"' The food of John the Baptist was the fruit of the locust tree and wild honey, and the disciples were forbidden to eat flesh food: 'Eat that which is set before you, but of that which is gotten by taking life, touch not, for it is not lawful to you. And into whatsoever city ye enter and they receive you, eat such things as are set before you without taking of life

'... And in the same house remain, eating and drinking such things as they give without shedding of blood ... Be ye therefore considerate, be tender, be pitiful, be kind; not to your kind alone, but to every creature which is within your care; for ye are to them as gods, to whom they look in their needs.'

It is interesting that the story of the miracle of the loaves and fishes is lacking in this translation. Instead there is a tale of the miracle of the bread and the fruit, and a pitcher of water. 'And Jesus set the bread and the fruit before them and also the water. And they did eat and drink and were filled. And they marvelled; for each had enough to spare, and there were four thousand.' And when Judas brings a lamb to be slain for the Passover, Jesus reproves him: 'Not by shedding innocent blood, but by living a righteous life shall ye find the peace of God ... Blessed are they who keep this law; for God is manifested in all creatures. All creatures live in God, and God is hid in them ... They in every nation who defile not themselves with cruelty, who do righteousness, love mercy, and revere all the works of God, who give succour to all that are weak and oppressed – the same are the Israel of God.'

Jesus was accused of speaking against the law when he quoted Jeremiah's words against blood offerings and sacrifices, and he answered his critics: 'Against Moses indeed I do not speak, nor against the law, which he permitted for the hardness of your hearts,' continuing:

> For the fruit of the trees and the seeds and of the herbs alone do I partake, and these are changed by the spirit into my flesh and blood. Of these alone and their like shall ye eat who believe in me and are my disciples; for of these, in the spirit, come life and health and healing unto man ...

If these excerpts are accepted as proof of nothing more, they at least confirm that the Bible was originally a much more comprehensive document than we have today. It would appear there were no discrepancies between the teachings of Jesus and the philosophy of humane vegetarianism, and it is unreasonable to expect there to be, for Jesus is known to have been a Nazarene – a pre-Christian sect of Syrian Jews similar to the Essenes whose obedience to the Laws of Moses took particular account of the commandment 'Thou shalt not kill.' Their inner orders abstained from both flesh-meats and alcohol.

But it is always skating on uncertain ice to resort to lifting passages out of their context. What must influence any responsible student concerned with the specifically Christian attitude to cruelty is not what paragraphs may be quoted from the Bible, nor what the interpretations of churchmen may be, but the whole spirit and tenor of Jesus's life so far as we are able to judge it from the texts that have come down to us. Whatever his personal failings and inconsistencies may have been, Jesus Christ was clearly a man who preached non-violence. The extent to which he was able to give attention to the matter of man's violence to other species is not known to us, and it may well be that he found quite enough to do in his short life to convince human beings of the basics of better conduct between themselves. 2000 years later, with the spade work of theory having long been completed, it is easier for us to broaden our concern, which is presumably precisely what Jesus and other great teachers have always expected their 'flocks' to do. Because few of them produced a specific Animals' Charter, we have no right to assume that the lower orders of creation would have been excluded from their compassion. How much more strange had that been the case! 'I say unto you, any cruelty or suffering you may wish to inflict upon animals, this you may do.' It somehow sounds unlikely.

But while the Bible may be the most important souce of guidance for Western people who feel the need for religious guidelines before being willing to question mankind's cruelty to animals, perhaps the main cradle of a more humane concern lay in the Far East. But although in general modern India, Sri Lanka, Burma and Thailand are vegetarian, Tibet and Japan are not, although Zen monks are among the exceptions and might have been expected to disseminate a wider interpretation of what must seem to many the unfortunately inconsistent doctrine of *ahimsa* ('non-killing'). The orthodox Hindu is vegetarian, but although Buddhists are forbidden to take life, *ahimsa* subscribing to the belief that all life is sacred and that it is man's duty to abstain from harming any living creature, less conscientious Buddhists have for long eaten meat if provided by another. There is even a sutta in the Buddhist scriptures where the Buddha flatly refused to make a strict rule that his monks must be vegetarian on the ground that the *more* strict rule was that they should take and eat whatever was put into their bowls when they went round begging. However, as the eminent Judge Christmas Humphreys, founder and president of The Buddhist Society, has pointed out, since what was given to them would almost certainly be rice and vegetables, the effect on their eating habits cannot have been great.[1]

Furthermore, it should be remembered that Buddhism is second not even to the Holy Bible in the number of interpretations it offers and invites. 'Buddha' is a title (meaning in the Sanskrit 'enlightened,' or 'to wake', and equating with Supreme Truth), not the name of a person, and although it is particularly and generally applied to Gautama, the historical founder of Buddhism, it is equally applicable to literally thousands of other teachers, especially in the field of Mahayana Buddhism which subscribes to countless Buddhas and Bodhisattvas (beings who present ideals of life and

135

embodiments of compassion, sometimes loosely called 'Buddhas of Compassion'). Mahayana (meaning 'Great vehicle') is the major part of Buddhism and evolved at about the beginning of the Christian era, adding its scriptures to (but not opposing) the Hinayana ('small vehicle') that represented the earliest school of Buddhism (now found only in the Theravada).

Just as 'The Buddha' is equated with Gautama, so is Gautama with the *Dhammapada* (The Path of the Buddha's Dhamma, or Teaching). The Pali version can be read in several English translations, and perhaps this is the best way to judge Gautama's actual attitude to taking life, bearing in mind that the Mahayana scriptures have appeared in Sanskrit, Chinese and other languages for the edification of a world population of Buddhists today estimated to be in the region of 400 million. One sect of the northern (Mahayana) Buddhists were the Shakyas (thought to have lived on the Indian side of the borders of Nepal in the Himalayan foothills), and their scriptural authority was one that left no doubt as to the 'Lord of Compassion's' views on eating meat. The Shakyamuni (Sanskrit, meaning 'the sage of the Shakyas', and a title of Gautama) Buddha says loud and clear:

> To avoid causing terror to living beings, let the Disciple refrain from eating meat ... the food of the wise is that which is consumed by the Sadhus (Yogis); it does not consist of meat ... there may be some foolish people in the future who will say that I permitted meat-eating and that I partook of meat myself, but ... meat-eating I have not permitted to anyone, I do not permit, I will not permit ... meat-eating in any form, in any manner, and in any place, is unconditionally and once and for all prohibited for all.

And one could hardly say it more flatly than that. However, the incursion of Western values has undoubtedly contributed to some unfortunate broadening of The Middle Path concept, and many Buddhists have extended their eating patterns well beyond the original tenets of their religious belief.

The doctrine of *ahimsa* was developed even more rigorously by the Jains, some one and a half million of whom are to be found in India today. Both monks and the laity are forbidden to eat meat, and this concern with the avoidance of taking life extends to hunting and agriculture. A text in many Jain temples reads: 'Non-violence is the highest religion.' Some Jains go so far as to breathe through closely woven cloth in case they swallow an insect, and the simple act of walking is seen, logically enough, as of equal danger to the smaller forms of life. Such extremes of concern are admirable, but for most of us they are likely to remain only a salutary reminder of the ideal.[2]

The contribution made by the Brahmanas of India should also be noted, and although the monotheistic traditions that developed west of the Indus tended to discourage ideas of compassion towards animals, some Muslim Sufi mystics (who came to be regarded as the Muslims' spiritual leaders) stressed the necessity for a fleshless diet for those hoping to achieve spiritual growth.

But the Bible and the ancient religious systems of the Far East are by no means the only source of early concern for the rights of beasts. Throughout history perhaps no country or religion has failed to develop some degree of ethical or ascetically-based realisation of man's relationship to other species. Ancient Greece and Egypt were aware of the religious form of vegetarianism, and their myths, like the earliest Hebrew, represented man as having been originally a fruit-eating creature. We now know from our study of physiology and history that these myths were not myths at all, and that men of the stature of Pythagoras, Plato, Diogenes, Ovid, Virgil, Seneca, Porphyry, Plotinus, Plutarch, Horace and Socrates, all of whom advocated a non-flesh diet, were the intuitive and reasonable counterparts of the scientifically knowledgeable modern man who has at last begun to realise that a meat diet is not only unnecessary but, on so many counts, positively inadvisable and unnatural to 'the terminal form of hominoidea' (ourselves). Those who can see only a divide between philosophy and science should notice how often they reach the same conclusions.

But neither the religious nor the secular history of vegetarianism can be covered in a single chapter. To provide anything like a correct and comprehensive account of the humane movement in the Western world alone, one must take into consideration the humanitarianism of Pythagoras, and later of the Platonists and neo-Platonists, which sprang directly from their superior philosophy of harmlessness, mercy and compassion that stemmed through the teachings of Empedocles, Plato and Philo to the Essenes – the sect from which Jesus gained much of his wisdom. Only a revival of this philosophy, opposed and persecuted by the Church and banished by Justinian when he closed the Academy of Athens where it had been preserved, will change the minds and hearts of those who refuse to accept what has not been blessed by the mouthpieces of orthodox Christianity.

THE MORE RECENT PAST

The darkest ages eventually detect a dawn. In Europe by the seventeenth and eighteenth centuries there was to be seen a renewal of confidence in the power and potentialities of moral progress, this humanitarianism (a term which, strictly speaking, denotes devotion to humanity rather than life in general, but has a wider connotation with humaneness) bringing some revival of sensitivity towards animal suffering. The Pythagorean attitude to flesh-eating was again called to mind, and numerous philosophers and men of letters wrote powerfully against mankind's callousness to the 'brute creation'.

Professor Duncan Williams, a teacher of seventeenth- and eighteenth-century literature, has made a notable contribution to our understanding of the humanising influence in the writings of that period in his book *Trousered Apes*. It makes a better introduction to the subject than I have room or ability to attempt here.

All through history it has been the proddings and promptings of concerned writers and speakers that have produced and strengthened those religions and organisations, sects and groups, that have advocated, either officially or unofficially, a vegetarian diet. Just as the organisational structure for Western vegetarianism was brought about in the main by a handful of Bible Christians, so has a minority of articulate people been essential to such well-known and more obscure orders as The Adventist Church; The American Natural Hygiene Society; the Dadupanthi Sadus; the Doukhobors; the Essene faith; the Liberal Catholic Church; The Order of the Cross; the Carthusian, St Benedict and Trappist orders of the Roman Catholic Church; the Rosicrusian Fellowship; The Salvation Army; the Swami Narang and Vishnoi sects; Taoists; The Theosophical Society; Tolstoyans; the Unity Church; and the Universal Christian Gnostic Movement.

But as we have seen, the secular arguments – for all that they may have been prompted by, and will always be the stronger for, philosophic reasoning and religious conviction – are in themselves all that is needed for any open-minded person to judge the strength of the case against cruelty to animals. When Plutarch wrote:

> The obligations of law and equity reach only to mankind, but kindness and beneficence should be extended to the creatures of every species, and these will flow from the breast of a true man, as streams that issue from the living fountain,

and was echoed many centuries later by Addison:

> True benevolence, or compassion, extends itself through the whole of existence, and sympathises with the distress of every creature capable of sensation. Little minds may be apt to consider compassion of this kind as an instance of weakness; but it is undoubtedly the evidence of a noble nature,

they spoke for the thinking and feeling people who have been found in even the most barbarous eras of our history. So many similar sentiments could be quoted, from Hesiod (in the eighth century BC) to the present day, that only the most stubborn or obtuse man could deny that many of the best minds known to civilisation have come down uncompromisingly against mankind's long and hideous history of almost unrelieved inhumanity towards the creatures unfortunate enough to share this planet with us.

Leo Tolstoy, who was less than happy that the world wished to honour him for little but his fictional work (which he saw as of infinitely less importance than his religious, social and political writings), was one of the most powerful critics of man's brutality towards other species. In 'The First Step' (*Essays and Letters*) he describes how, when he was walking near Moscow, he saw a pig with its throat already gashed, running away from its slaughterers, only to be caught and finished off. The 'strong, red, coarse carman' who was giving Tolstoy a lift sighed when the pig's squeals had ceased, and asked Tolstoy: 'Do men really have to answer for such things?' Tolstoy comments: 'So strong is man's aversion to all killing. But by example, by encouraging greediness, by the assertion that God has allowed it, and, above all, by habit, people entirely lose this natural feeling.'

Much of 'The First Step' is given over to slaughter-house descriptions, for Tolstoy was no squeamish theorist. These are no more horrifying than scenes that can be witnessed to this day and every day in abattoirs all over the world, for all that the so-called humane killer and other aids (usually more to do with cleanliness and economics than with humanity) are employed, here and there, to placate the as yet hardly visible stirrings of mankind's conscience. Tolstoy rounds off the essay, which was written as Preface to a Russian translation of *The Ethics of Diet*, with an unanswerable argument for vegetarianism that includes the following lines:

> ... if a man's aspirations towards right living are serious ... he will first abstain from animal food because ... its use is simply immoral, as it requires the performance of an act which is contrary to moral feeling – killing; and is called forth only by greed and the desire for tasty food.

Tolstoy's objection to cruelty was religiously centred and he rejoiced that the vegetarian movement indicated an evolutionary trend in mankind:

> This movement should bring particular joy to those concerned with bringing about the kingdom of God on earth ... because vegetarianism is a sign that the aspiration of mankind towards moral perfection is serious and sincere.

Tolstoy, of course, was looking at a movement that had not yet been seriously infiltrated by those whose concern was that a fleshless diet might bring them better health rather than that it prevented the breeding and suffering of animals. Before our awareness of the facts of physiology and nutrition spurred the realisation that a natural diet was obviously healthier than one suiting a different species, nearly all the great writers and philosophers of the past took a primarily ethical stand against the exploitation of animals. Plutarch, who has already been quoted, in his 'Essay on Flesh Eating' laboured both the non-necessity and the cruelty of the habit:

> Man makes use of flesh not out of want and necessity, seeing that he has the liberty to make his choice of herbs and fruits, the plenty of which is inexhaustible; but out of

luxury, and being cloyed with necessaries, he seeks after impure and inconvenient diet, purchased by the slaughter of living beasts; by showing himself more cruel than the most savage of wild beasts.

'Inconvenient' has become a curiously appropriate term now that the uneconomic facts of obtaining protein through the bodies of animals have begun to be brought home to us. It is the continued applicability of their statements to the modern situation that makes the words of past writers and philosophers of such particular interest today. Even in Roman times man's cowardice in aping the majority was held in contempt by those of freer minds. Seneca wrote:

> If true, the Pythagorean principles as to abstaining from flesh, foster innocence; if ill-founded they at least teach us frugality, and what loss have you in losing your cruelty? It merely deprives you of the food of lions and vultures. We shall recover our sound reason only if we separate ourselves from the herd ... the very fact of the approbation of the multitude is a proof of the unsoundness of the opinion or practice; let us ask what is best – not what is customary. Let us love temperance – let us be just – let us refrain from bloodshed.

It is unfortunate that some men of our times who have *known* better have not necessarily had the courage to act upon what they knew. Even Albert Schweitzer, who could write: 'Reverence for life affords my fundamental principle – good consists in maintaining, assisting and enhancing life, and to destroy, to harm or to hinder life is evil,' wobbled a bit at dinner and could temporise with: 'I am conscious that flesh-eating is not in accordance with the finer feelings and I abstain therefrom whenever I can.' However, he was in no doubt that in time all wobblers would accept that:

> Slowly in our European thought comes the notion that ethics has not only to do with mankind but with the animal creation as well. This begins with St Francis of Assisi. The explanation which applies only to man must be given up. Thus we shall arrive at saying that ethics is reverence for *all* life.

And that he was moving towards a more consistent pattern is suggested by his unequivocal statement that:

> The great fault of all ethics hitherto has been that they believed themselves to have to deal only with the relations of man to man. In reality, however, the question is what is his attitude to the world and all life that comes within his reach. A man is ethical only when life, as such, is sacred to him, that of plants and animals as that of his fellow men, and when he devotes himself helpfully to all life that is in need of help.

Einstein, also, agreed with the aim of vegetarianism for aesthetic and moral reasons, affirming that 'it is my view that a vegetarian manner of living by purely physical effect on the human temperament would most beneficially influence the lot of mankind', but like Dean Inge, Byron, von Haller, Paley, Chesterfield and many others he failed to live up to this realisation to the same extent as his contemporary, the greatest exponent of non-violence on all levels, Mahatma Gandhi whose statement 'I hold flesh-food to be unsuited to our species. We err in copying the lower animal world . . . if we are superior to it' is only to give a passing glance to the views of this remarkable man. 'The basis of my vegetarianism is not physical, but moral . . . I would love to think that all of us who called ourselves vegetarians should have that basis.'

The principle of *ahimsa* (non-violence) was so much a part of Gandhi's outlook, and so taken for granted in India, that little of his thought except on a political level has filtered through to the West. A bridge between modern East and West has to some extent been maintained by such excellent journals as the London-based monthly *The Aryan Path*, the Indian monthlies *Mira* and *Sarvodaya*, and the quarterly *Gandhi Marg* (journal of the Gandhi Peace Foundation). Individuals of the stature of Vinoba Bhave, Jayaprakash Narayan, T. L. and J. P. Vaswani, and Sophia Wadia have in their different ways contributed greatly, both to the emancipation of their country from the threatening bondage of Western materialism and to keeping alive the flow of humane and humanitarian thought without which the West is in danger of regarding everywhere east of Suez as being territory only of interest to economists and tradesmen. Sadly, however, all too little of the essence of Eastern belief in man's obligations to the animal kingdom filters through to the West.

In recent years, numerous British and American writers have expressed with power and feeling their concern with mankind's continued brutality and insensitivity. But although some excellent condemnations of vivisection and other experiments on animals have been produced (particularly to be recommended are *In Pity and in Anger* and *The Dark Face of Science* by John Vyvyan), and despite quite a number of books on 'factory-farming' (Ruth Harrison's *Animal Machines* is the 'classic') and the blood-sports, singularly few full-length studies of our largest-scale cruelty to animals have achieved publication. There have been some excellent books of a general nature from which one would suppose a more compassionate regard for sentient food sources must be the logical corollary (Duncan Williams' *Trousered Apes* is a superb example), but for a more direct and unequivocal concern there are few to be found other than Henry Bailey Stevens' *The Recovery of Culture*, Roy Walker's *The Golden Feast*, Frank Avray Wilson's *Food for the Golden Age*, and some anthologies of shorter contributions. Two highly informative and crisp studies of vegetarianism from Britain and America are Geoffrey Rudd's *Why Kill for Food?* and Nathaniel Altman's *Eating for Life*, but while both are extremely good so far as they go, they do not pretend to present more than the basic facts in a brief and readable form. A very useful general work was Charles D.

Niven's *History of the Humane Movement*, but its coverage of the historical background is deficient in a number of important respects, and the concern with food animals seems to be more with how best they may be slaughtered relatively humanely rather than with whether they should be slaughtered at all. *All Heaven in a Rage* by E. S. Turner is another excellent general study, showing how the British race was shamed and legislated into moderating some of its cruelties, but there is a weakness about the author's discussion of flesh-eating that invites suspicion that beyond a certain point, like Schopenhauer and some others, mind proved subservient to stomach. For those for whom brain and stomach are working in harmony, the number of vegetarian cookery books now available must almost rival what has been produced in that ecological field to which vegetarianism is now seen to be so relevant.

Such recent books are only the tip of an iceberg more than 2000 years old. Strangely, some of the most outspoken critics have had interests and affiliations that one might suppose would preclude the championing of 'mere' animals. A number of high-ranking members of the armed services, for instance, have been particularly prominent in their criticisms, and even Cardinal Newman – whose Church, sadly, must be numbered among those least concerned with the subservience of the animal kingdom to the whims and greeds of mankind – showed an anger that, although prompted by the barbarities of vivisection, could only logically be applied to all forms of exploitation and cruelty to animals:

> Now what is it moves our very heart, and sickens us so much at the cruelty shown to poor brutes? I suppose this; first, that they have done us no harm; next, that they have no power whatever to resistance; it is the cowardice and tyranny of which they are the victims which make their sufferings so especially touching; ... there is something so very dreadful, so Satanic in tormenting those who have never harmed us, and who cannot defend themselves, who are utterly in our power.

I am tempted to end this section with a list of living and very recent writers, philosophers, theologians, scientists, teachers and others who have advocated and to varying degrees followed a meat-free diet. From the recent past people of the stature of William Booth, Krishnamurti, Annie Besant, Isaac Pitman, H. G. Wells, Upton Sinclair and Todd Ferrier spring to mind. But the list of both recent and modern names would be endless and, inevitably, invidious. In any case, no one who needs a who's who of humane concern is a very hopeful candidate for change; he might do better to consider the environmental and economic arguments. But for those who wish to dig further into the historical background to, and the literature of, vegetarianism, the following roll of past names (which excludes most of those mentioned elsewhere in this book) offers a useful nucleus:

Apollonius; Akbar; Asoka; Athanasius; Akhnaton; Jacques Bossuet; George Cheyne; John Chrysostom; Clement of Alexandria; Antonio Cocchi; Luigi Cornaro;

Charles Darwin; George Daumer; St David; Rukmini Devi; Ralph Waldo Emerson; Epicurus; John Evelyn; Benjamin Franklin; Pierre Gassendi; Jean Antoine Gleizès; David Hartley; Christian Wilhelm Hufeland; Anna Kingsford; Alphonse Lamartine; William Lambe; Justus von Liebig; Carl Linné (Linnaeus); Mahavira; Bernard de Mandeville; Jules Michelet; John Milton; Montaigne; General C. Montgomery; Thomas More; Isaac Newton; John Frank Newton; John Oswald; Origen; Richard Phillips; Alexander Pope; John Ray; Joseph Ritson; J.-J. Rousseau; William Shakespeare; Gustav von Struve; Emanuel Swedenborg; Rabindranath Tagore; Tertullian; James Thomson; Hermes Trismegistus; Leonardo da Vinci; Francois Voltaire; Richard Wagner; John Wesley; Zoroaster.

Since this book first appeared, Janet Barkas has published an engaging and informative history of the vegetarian state of mind, entitled *The Vegetable Passion*.

To round off the picture, it is necessary to describe briefly how the present organisational structural of vegetarianism came into being and to identify the principal societies, etc., in America and the United Kingdom. This information is to be found in Appendix I to this book.

IN SUMMARY

This has had to be a short chapter, but it may have given some idea of the considerable historical, literary and organisational ramifications of what (for lack of a better single word) is called vegetarianism. Perhaps one day someone will bring together the main writings of those who have been moved to protest against our treatment of the creatures we have chosen to eat.

What has been said is of more importance than who has said it, and the point to emphasise is that, so far from the principles of abstaining from flesh-eating being the province of a handful of eccentrics, many volumes could be filled with the sane, compassionate and often angry statements of men and women in all walks of life and of all degrees of eminence and perception who have broken through the apathy barrier into a shocked awareness of the sheer scale of our brutality to lesser creatures. Their comments can be read by anyone sufficiently concerned to do a little research.

Sadly, few but those already half way towards a more humane attitude of mind can be bothered to seek the opinions that have been expressed on the least admirable aspects of mankind's history. The most popular writers are those who bolster up our weaknesses, gloss over or openly justify and even glamorise our cruelties, and offer the same recipe as before. Even those usually more sensitive and civilised writers such as the poets and philosophers tend to be remembered mainly for their least demanding exhortations. How many people know, for instance, that Shelley wrote a powerful treatise on the vegetable system of diet in which he put forward scientific and humane arguments that can hardly be improved upon today? But as Howard Williams wrote in 1883:

> That a principle of profound significance for the welfare of our own species in particular, and for the peaceful harmony of the world in general – a true spiritualism, of which some of the most admirable of the poets of the pre-Christian ages proved themselves not unconscious – has been, for the most part, altogether overlooked or ignored by modern aspirants to poetic fame, is matter for our gravest lament. Thomson, Pope, Shelley, Lamartine – to whom Milton, perhaps, may be added – these form a small band who almost alone represent, and have developed the earlier inspiration of, a Hesiod, Ovid or Virgil, the prophet-poets who, faithful to their proper calling, have sought to *unbarbarise* and elevate human life by arousing, in various degrees, feelings of horror and aversion from the prevailing materialism of living.

Yet today there is a detectable and significant reaction against that materialism. The mounting interest in natural foods and particularly the vegetarian and vegan diets is world-wide and especially noticeable among the young who are the sternest critics of our materialism. It may well be they, and the environmental and economic factors that cannot be ignored in our over-populated, violent and crisis-ridden world, who are combining to transmute the history of vegetarianism into a humane, healthy, inexpensive and practical way of life.

Notes

1. Another non-story, which appears in the Pali Canon and is often quoted by Western people anxious to prove that Eastern nations are no less insensitive to animals' suffering than they are themselves, is that Buddha died after eating tainted pork. However, as scholars have pointed out, the term 'tainted pork' has an obvious symbolic meaning, concerning the much older tradition that the Buddha gave out too much and brought about the tremendous reaction of the Brahmins against his rashness. Delving into such legends achieves little, especially when language, metaphor and parable do so much to confuse the issue (the word 'pork', for instance, can mean 'esoteric teaching'!), and once again one must take into account the whole spirit and tone of a prophet's life and teachings rather than pick on his isolated remarks, or on those of his alleged spokesmen. As Christmas Humphreys has remarked, 'one cannot imagine the world's greatest teacher eating meat, or for that matter, not knowing that what he ate was tainted'.
2. Of the many factors that are responsible for the continuation of the caste-system in India, one is the differences in diet. Acharya Vinobaji has said (*Sarvodaya*, October 1973): 'Out of the 25 million people in Gujarat, 20 millions do not eat meat. The businessmen of Rajasthan and all the Jains of India abstain from it. The Shaivas, Vaishnavas and Brahmins of Maharashtra, Karnatak, Andrha, Tamilnadu and Kerala do not take meat. Thus at least 50 millions out of India's 550 millions never taste meat. Among the rest who do, about 250 millions take it once a week or on festival occasions. Very few have it as a regular meal every day.' He suggests that only a wide acceptance of vegetarianism can bring about a reduction in casteism.

Postscript

THE United Nations World Food Conference took place in November 1974 after this book was written. Although the outcome left much to be desired, the Conference's debate on the international food crisis prompted renewed attention from many quarters, ranging from such admissions from nutritionists that even 2800 calories and 65 g of protein may be far more than most of us need, to forthright statements from economists on the sheer wastefulness of rearing animals for human food. No less a platform than *The Economist* has given prominence to the view that we can no longer afford to use 7 tons of cereal to produce 1 ton of beef, and in the issue of 2.11.1974 Barbara Ward gave some telling statistics on this vital concern in her article 'the fat years and the lean':

> 'North America's annual consumption per head increased (in the 1960's) from about 1000 lb to nearly 1900 lb of cereals – and all but 150 lb of it, through the conversion of animal feeding stuffs, in meat and poultry. Western Europe and the Soviet Union followed on behind. By 1972, at least a third of the world's increased demand for food reflected increases not in population but in affluent diets.
>
> By the time mechanisation, fertiliser, pesticides, transport, processing and super-marketing are added in, at least five units of energy (kilocalories) have been invested to produce one unit of energy in the consumer's actual diet. Changing patterns of demand to higher protein diets have also encouraged the more intensive use of energy. Processing cereals through farm animals not only uses more cereals. It lengthens and increases energy-intensive patterns of production.
>
> The Soviet Union is as committed as any other bourgeois society to the maintenance of meat eating, if necessary by massive purchase of animal feeding stuffs abroad.
>
> Since 1965, Americans have added 350 lb per head to their annual diet, largely in the form of beef and poultry. This is very nearly the equivalent of an Indian's diet for a whole year. Europeans and Russians are not far behind the Americans.'

In *Can Britain Feed Itself?* Dr Kenneth Mellanby has pointed out that nearly 90 per cent of Britain's 46,919,000 acres of agricultural land goes to support the huge livestock population of 195½ million – 14½ million cattle, 28 million sheep, 9 million pigs, 144 million poultry. 'Not only do they use the grazing land of 29 million acres, but three quarters of the acreage of tillage is sown with crops for livestock. In addition, many tons of animal feed are imported, much of it from countries where human malnutrition and starvation are rife. When we consume a large steak, we are eating something that may have used enough grain to keep a family in drought-stricken areas of Africa for a week.'

But while on the one hand the food-processing industry – and particularly the meat processors – are now waiting for the green light in the form of new legislation which is essential before the real benefits of using textured proteins on a wider scale can be exploited, on the other are ranged the diehards and the vested interests who cherish the status quo. In September 1975 British butchers and farmers started a campaign to persuade people to eat even more meat, and in time to pay more for it, while in support of this lamentable disinclination to face the basic needs of our day the Ministry of Agriculture confirmed that the Government and EEC were prepared to spend £135 million in that coming year on helping British beef farmers.

The food we may be eating in the future, therefore, is now a major subject for debate. Some desperate manipulations of statistics have tried to prove that meat-eating societies need not fear worse than a reduction in their consumption of animal products. In the short term, this may well be so. But as long-cherished notions of the essential and desirable nature of a meat-based economy topple daily in the face of mankind's mounting problems of material survival, the luxury of self-deception giving way to the stark necessity to face facts, it would seem that whatever changes lie ahead, they are likely to confirm the central argument of this book.

In revising the text for this latest edition (1979) I have concentrated on matters of fact. Statistics and other technical data have not been replaced unless more recent figures have shown a substantially altered picture.

The main arguments originally presented would seem to have been strengthened by recent findings and admissions, and it seems unlikely that the principal reasons for adopting a more humane diet will prompt serious qualification or denial in the foreseeable future.

Appendix I

THE eighteenth century brought a new feeling for the styles and values of the classical world. Though much of this interest was centred on the more visible aspects such as architecture and the arts, the literature of the period could hardly fail to acknowledge the humanising influence in the cultures of Greece and Italy. It was not, however, until the nineteenth century that a more humane way of thinking gave birth to an identifiable philosophy and structure.

By 1842 the word 'vegetarian' came into use, and in 1847 the first secular organisation to promote a fleshless diet was formed. It was called The Vegetarian Society and was founded in Manchester, England, owing its existence in large measure to members of the Bible Christian Church founded in Salford in 1809 by a young Anglican clergyman with the somewhat inappropriate name of William Cowherd. Cowherd believed that total abstinence from flesh foods was necessary for spiritual growth, and his congregation pledged themselves to be vegetarian. So convinced were the Bible Christians of their mission that forty-one of them, under the leadership of the Rev. William Metcalfe, emigrated to America, and established a similar Church in Philadelphia. Their numbers steadily increased and their philosophy was strengthened by the support of such men as Dr Reuben D. Mussey (fourth president of the American Medical Association) and the Rev. Sylvester Graham whose research in grains led to the use of the flour of that name for baking. J. H. Kellogg, MD, was another strict vegetarian and supported the American vegetarian movement with much enthusiasm.

In 1908 the world's largest vegetarian organisation, the International Vegetarian Union, was founded, and today it has branches throughout the world. The vegetarian societies of England and America, with their vegan counterparts, are now flourishing as never before and can supply information on all aspects of vegetarian practice and belief. The Science Council of the IVU abstracts from scientific journals material concerned with nutritional and agricultural developments that are consistent with the ethical standards of vegetarianism. In Europe, Scandinavia, Australasia and elsewhere, vegetarian societies are also finding evidence of the mounting interest in a more truly civilised pattern of eating.

In 1971 the bi-monthly organ of The Vegetarian Society (UK) Ltd (with headquarters in Altrincham, Cheshire, and offices in Marloes Road,

London), *The British Vegetarian*, changed its name to *The Vegetarian* and is now (1979) published every other month as *Alive*. This enjoys a considerably wider circulation and achieves a high level of journalism. Of more sober format, but of great value for its presentation of both factual and ethical/philosophical matter, is the quarterly journal *The Vegan*, issued by The Vegan Society of 47 Highlands Road, Leatherhead, Surrey. In America, The American Vegan Society of Malaga, New Jersey, also puts out some valuable literature. The American Vegetarian Union promotes the better-known lacto-vegetarian way of life. As some indication that in America too the interest in vegetarianism is on the increase, it has been estimated that the total number of vegetarians in the United States is nearing the 3,000,000 mark. Sadly, a great number of these have been prompted mainly by concern for their personal health, but to redress this balance somewhat America can boast at least one development that appears to have no parallel in the United Kingdom. As long ago as 1911 an American woman, M. R. L. Freshel, founded what was then a unique organisation inasmuch as it was dedicated to the prevention of all exploitation of, and cruelty to, animals. She called it The Millenium Guild. But it was not until she met George Bernard Shaw, who became her close friend for the last forty years of his life, that Emarel (as Shaw called her) accepted that a consistent concern for animal welfare cannot exclude the many cruelties involved in eating their flesh. After she died in 1948 at the age of eighty-four her husband Curtis P. Freshel, a great grandson of Edward VII, assumed the Presidency, continuing to distribute its textbook and ensuring a constant flow to all parts of the world of professionally presented humane writing mostly in the form of the well-known Millenium Guild pamphlets and leaflets, as well as through press advertising. But perhaps the chief and most permanent contribution made to the humane 'Cause' by the Millenium Guild since 1948 was the establishment of the M. R. L. Freshel Award for the most outstanding humanitarian book of the year, the monetary prize being designed to encourage and propagate work of the highest literary quality by professional writers who stood to lose financially by writing on a theme of so little general interest in a society overwhelmingly unconcerned by the suffering of animals bred and slaughtered for our tables.

To date, the Award has been given to Professor Henry Bailey Stevens for his remarkable book *The Recovery of Culture*, to Roy Walker for his magnificent anthology *The Golden Feast*, to Upton Ewing for *The Essene Christ*, to Richard St Barbe Baker for *Sahara Conquest*, and on two occasions to Esmé Wynne-Tyson, the last Award being for her book *The Philosophy of Compassion*.

Appendix II

Sir Arthur Knight, chairman of Courtaulds Limited, one of the companies who have entered the expanding market for textured vegetable proteins, has kindly supplied the following lecture-notes on the economics of man-made fibres and their development in the nutritional field.

The essential process characteristics [of Courtauld's TVP products 'Vegex,' 'Kesp', etc.] are extraordinarily like those applicable to the man-made fibres. These, too, initially had to establish themselves against the entrenched natural fibres based, like food production, on agricultural processes. In the pre-1914 years before man-made fibres were established commercially, cotton and wool were the only textile fibres. In this country they now account for only 46 per cent of the fibres consumed, and we have a man-made fibre output of well over 600,000 tons a year, of which nearly 500,000 tons are used in the domestic market. Interestingly, I am told that this country's meat consumption is about 3 million tons a year, so the scale factors for the edible spun protein product will be similar to those for man-made fibres as soon as its use is established.

One of the man-made fibres which accounts for about one-third of the output is viscose staple. This was developed in the late 1930s. Its selling price in those years can be expressed as a ratio of the comparable cotton price at 100; for the years 1969 to 1971, after more than 30 years of development, the comparable ratio is 45. This is a measure of the extent to which the man-made product has become cheaper, relative to the natural product.

Another group of man-made fibres accounting for something like one-sixth of the UK output are the acrylic fibres. These have been developed more recently, in the late 50's and early 60's. Their price can be compared more sensibly with that of wool. If the 1959–61 price ratio is taken as 100, the comparable ratio for 1969–71 is 60. Here again we have a measure of the extent to which, with increased volume and experience, the man-made product has increased its competitive advantage. By taking average prices over three-year periods I have attempted to eliminate the passing effect of the wide fluctuations which occur from time to time in the prices of the natural products.

Nobody would be so unwise as to predict similar developments in the edible spun protein field when compared with the natural product, either in terms of volume or in terms of price. All I am saying is that the basic

149

economic and technological factors would support a similar development.

We are concerned with manufacturing processes which offer the opportunity for considerable cost reductions as the volume of output increases – a field in which the skills of the chemical engineer find their scope. One of the American consulting firms talks of experience curves and claims that cost reductions of typically 20–30 per cent can be expected with each doubling of accumulated experience (annual output figures are a good measure of this). This concept includes scale economies – those cost reductions which result from using the technical processes appropriate to the size of output which is being planned. It also includes the economies which result from reducing the number of changes to the production line which are needed to cater for the variety the market needs.

Another source of these economies arises from the ability with experience to design increments to original plants at capital costs per unit of output well below the original. It follows from this that the industries in which these economies are greatest are those in which the large firms have advantages – which include their ability to raise the large sums needed for investment.

Agricultural processes are essentially batch methods. The processes which we are developing for edible spun proteins are essentially continuous. The scale effects of increasing volume with a continuous process give an inherent advantage as against any batch process. The Ministry of Agriculture have stated that between 1958 and 1967 labour productivity in agriculture grew at about 7 per cent a year and this reflects the big improvements which have taken place in British agriculture in recent years. But in Courtaulds, in presenting evidence to the Monopolies Commission, we were able to show that our labour productivity has improved over much longer periods at the rate of more than 10 per cent a year. The difference between these rates of improvement in productivity is what makes for the ultimate advantage of a chemical engineering type manufacturing process over the agricultural processes.

Other important characteristics of the products of the chemical engineering type industries are their relative price stability and the consistency of quality which it is possible to achieve.

Appendix III

SYMBOLS AND CONVERSION FACTORS

WEIGHT

microgram		μg	ounce		oz
milligram		mg	pound		lb
gram		g			
kilogram		kg			
1 g	=	1,000 mg	1 g	=	0·035 oz
	=	1,000,000 μg	1 kg	=	2·20 lb
1 kg	=	1,000 g	1 oz	=	28·35 g
			1 lb	=	453·6 g

ENERGY:

joule		J	kilocalorie		kcal
kilojoule		kJ			
megajoule		MJ			
1 kJ	=	1,000 J	1 kcal	=	4·19 kJ
1 MJ	=	1,000 kJ	1 MJ	=	239 kcal
	=	1,000,000 J			

VOLUME:

millilitre		ml	fluid ounce		fl oz
litre		l	pint		pt
1 l	=	1,000 ml	1 fl oz	=	28·4 ml
			1 pt	=	20 fl oz
			1 pt	=	568 ml

Bibliography

Altman, Nathaniel, *Eating for Life*, Theosophical Publishing House, 1973

Barkas, Janet, *The Vegetable Passion*, Routledge, 1975

Brophy, Brigid, *The Rights of Animals*, Sunday Times/Vegetarian Society, 1965

Clark, Stephen R. L., *The Moral Status of Animals*, Oxford U.P., 1977

Douglas, J. Sholto and Hart, A. de J., *Forest Farming*, Watkins, 1976

Godlovitch, S. & R. and Harris, John (eds), *Animals, Men and Morals*, Gollancz, 1971

Harrison, Ruth, *Animal Machines*, Vincent Stuart, 1964

Lewis, John and Towers, Bernard, *Naked Ape or Homo Sapiens?* Garnstone Press, 1972

Linzey, Andrew, *Animal Rights*, SCM Press, 1976

McCance, R. A. and Widdowson, E. M., *The Composition of Foods*, HMSO, 1973

Montagu, M. F. Ashley, *The Nature of Human Aggression*, Oxford U.P., 1976

Morris, R. K. and Fox, M. W. (eds), *On the Fifth Day: Animal Rights and Human Ethics*, Acropolis Books/Centaur Press, 1978

Nance, John, *The Gentle Tasaday*, Gollancz, 1975

Niven, Charles D., *History of the Humane Mov ement*, Johnson, 1967

Paterson, David and Ryder, Richard D. (eds), *Animals' Rights: a Symposium*, Centaur Press, 1979

Porphyry, *On Abstinence from Animal Food*, Centaur Press, 1965

Regan, Tom and Singer, Peter (eds), *Animal Rights and Human Obligations*, Prentice Hall, 1976

Roberts, Catherine, *The Scientific Conscience*, Centaur Press, 1974

Ryder, Richard D., *Victims of Science*, Davis-Poynter, 1975

Singer, Peter, *Animal Liberation*, Cape, 1976

Turner, E. S., *All Heaven in a Rage*, M. Joseph, 1964

Vyvyan, John, *In Pity and in Anger*, M. Joseph, 1969

Vyvyan, John, *The Dark Face of Science*, M. Joseph, 1971

Wilson, Frank, *Food Fit for Humans*, Daniel, 1975

Wynne-Tyson, Esmé, *The Philosophy of Compassion*, Centaur Press, 1970

Wynne-Tyson, Jon, *The Civilized Alternative*, Centaur Press, 1972

In this (1979) edition I have shortened the bibliography to show relatively recent and mostly available key works. A few are outside the strict concern of this book, particularly those on animal experimentation by Catherine Roberts, Richard Ryder and John Vyvyan; and on human nature and origins by Ashley Montagu, John Nance, John Lewis and Bernard Towers.

Other works, not listed in the bibliography, are mentioned in the body of the book, notably in chapter nine. There are many other fine works in the literature of animal welfare, most of them sadly unavailable except as rarities in the second-hand book market, such as Henry Salt's *Animals' Rights* (see George Hendrick's *Henry Salt: Humanitarian Reformer and Man of Letters*, University of Illinois Press, 1977) and Thomas Tryon's *Wisdom's Dictates, Good Housewife Made a Doctor*, and *Miscellania*.

I have removed from the bibliography a number of more recent works which are of only marginal relevance, though valuable in their own field, and may or may not be out of print. They include Doris Grant's *Your Daily Food* (Faber, 1975), Ivan Illich's *Medical Nemesis* (Calder & Boyars, 1975), Schopenhauer's *On the Basis of Morality* (Bobbs Merrill, 1965), and E. F. Schumacher's *A Guide for the Perplexed* (Cape, 1977), a book little concerned directly with animal welfare, but in my view of far more importance than his better-known *Small is Beautiful*.

Books dealing in the narrower sense with plant foods have had to be excluded, as have most of those in the more technical reaches of health, nutrition, anthropology and other scientific specialisms.

Among other sources of literature and direct action for the advancement of humane thought may be mentioned the Society for Animal Rights Inc., Clark's Summit, Pa., USA, and The Humane Society of the United States, Washington, D.C.

Index

Partly to discourage wrong conclusions being drawn from passages out of context, this index excludes certain entries – notably diseases, also most animals' names, foods, nutrients, and such broad categories as countries and religious systems, except for major references. The analysed Contents pages direct the reader to the main areas of discussion.

155

159

'A most important and timely book. This book is the most clear and comprehensive case for vegetarianism yet published. It gives all the reasons most clearly and cogently and, moreover, with a vitality and felicity of expression that makes the book an invigorating delight to read. . . . As a source book it is indispensable'
The Vegan

'He writes with a passionate conviction but backs every statement with enough facts to satisfy the most hard-headed statistic-seeker. Perhaps his most subtle achievement is the slow revelation that the arguments *for* meat-eating are in fact those that are emotional and irrational'
The Times

'Replete with dietetic information, valuable in itself whatever one's reaction to a vegan profession of faith'
Sunday Telegraph

'Jon Wynne-Tyson is an original thinker. Thus even those who have read everything written on the subject are going to find fresh, new insights. The quality of his writing is clear, succinct and compulsively readable'
The Vegetarian

'A strong, well-argued case'
Nutrition and Food Science

'Cogently argued and fully documented'
The Ecologist

CENTAUR PRESS

Distributed in the U K by
THORSONS PUBLISHERS LTD
Denington Estate Wellingborough
Northants NN8 2RQ

HEALTH AND MEDICINE/WORLD AFFAIRS   0 90000097 X